THROUGH FIRE *and grace*

RISING FROM THE DEPTHS OF DESPAIR TO LIVE A LIFE OF HOPE

BROOKE ANDERSEN

THROUGH FIRE and grace

Copyright © 2024 by Brooke Andersen

All rights reserved. No part of this publication may be reproduced, stored in a retrieval system, or transmitted in any form or by any means, electronic, mechanical, photocopying, recording, or otherwise, without written permission of the publisher or author, except for the use of brief quotations in a book review.

Although the author and publisher have made every effort to ensure that the information in this book was correct at press time, the author and publisher do not assume and hereby disclaim any liability to any party for any loss, damage, or disruption caused by errors or omissions, whether such errors or omissions result from negligence, accident, or any other cause.

Adherence to all applicable laws and regulations, including international, federal, state and local governing professional licensing, business practices, advertising, and all other aspects of doing business in the US, Canada or any other jurisdiction is the sole responsibility of the reader and consumer.

Neither the author nor the publisher assumes any responsibility or liability whatsoever on behalf of the consumer or reader of this material. Any perceived slight of any individual or organization is purely unintentional.

The resources in this book are provided for informational purposes only and should not be used to replace the specialized training and professional judgment of a health care or mental health care professional.

Neither the author nor the publisher can be held responsible for the use of the information provided within this book. Please always consult a trained professional before making any decision regarding treatment of yourself or others.

To request permissions, contact the publisher at publish@joapublishing.com

Hardcover ISBN: 978-1-961098-73-2
Paperback ISBN: 978-1-961098-72-5
eBook ISBN: 978-1-961098-74-9
Printed in the USA.

Joan of Arc Publishing
Meridian, ID 83646
www.joapublishing.com

Table of Contents

Introduction 1

Chapter 1: The Awakening 4

Chapter 2: The Desire for More 8

Chapter 3: Rape 12

Chapter 4: How Rape Affected My Marriage Bed 18

Chapter 5: How My Rape Affected My Husband 22

Chapter 6: Transitioning Faith 30

Chapter 7: Who is God? 40

Chapter 8: The Dark Side of Motherhood 45

Chapter 9: Mental Hospital 55

Chapter 10: Groundhog Day 61

Chapter 11: Journaling 65

Chapter 12: You Have More Choice than You Think You Do 81

Chapter 13: Choosing to Live 85

Chapter 14: Let's Talk Miracles 94

Chapter 15: The Path to Barcelona 101

Chapter 16: Selling the House 110

Chapter 17: God's Silence 115

Chapter 18: Purpose in Pain 120

Chapter 19: Comparison 127
Chapter 20: Grief of the Should-Have-Beens 131
Chapter 21: Prognosis Power.. 136
Chapter 22: Chronic Illness Identity... 141
Chapter 23: The Ultimate Betrayal... 158
Chapter 24: Healing is Written in Your Cells 167
Chapter 25: I Am Worthy.. 171
Chapter 26: Growth 175
Chapter 27: Authenticity = Safety and Healing......................... 182
Chapter 28: Waiting to be Healed to Live 188
Chapter 29: Phoenix Rising from the Ashes.............................. 193

Introduction

This book is written to those who feel alone, like nobody else has ever felt their level of despair before. To the ones struggling with chronic illness or their mental health. To those who feel stuck in a prison instead of experiencing life in their body. To those who want more for their life and feel called to be more.

To the people who feel life has thrown shitty curveballs.

I see you.

To the people experiencing *Groundhog Day*[1]—the same record on repeat—I say let's challenge the record playing and break the cycles. This book is here to awaken a part of you that you may have never experienced or was just beaten out of you.

In these pages, may you find comfort in not being alone. May you use this book as a guide on your path to healing and a beacon of hope in your dark moments.

---

[1] *Groundhog Day*, written by Danny Rubin and Harold Ramis, directed by Harold Ramis, starring Bill Murray, Andie McDowell, and Chris Elliot, released by Columbia Pictures February 4, 1993.

Lean into the discomfort that these pages may bring up for you. Let the emotion provide its teaching without judgment.

Let the words on these pages hold you. Hold your tears, your pain, your fear, your hope for the future. Let this book wake up the dreamer in you once again. Let it help you own your voice, to find your worth and know it!

Let me hold space in your pain and encourage you to step into your next chapter of life.

Here I have compiled anthems that have spoken to me in my darkest days. I found that through much of my postpartum psychosis I really didn't have words left to pray. I felt I had said them all, and music became my prayer. Journaling became my war cry. I will share with you here some of the songs that helped me through the darkest nights. May you listen to this music as you experience my book and find anthems for your own struggles, words in music to put into prayer. I would listen to songs and it was like my heart would just start pouring out to the heavens. The way the music felt and the words hit were the prayers.

To some who are reading this, life has felt unbearable. Like, what is the point? I know, I have been there. Feel the pain of the weight of this burden, let the music loosen the parasite of this belief, and know you are being held by me and by God in these pages.

INTRODUCTION

May you feel seen, heard, and understood. May you be willing to grow and heal and ultimately find the hope required to change your life.

Music

"Beautiful" —MercyMe

"Brave" —Sara Bareilles

"Do It Again" —Elevation Worship

"Even Then" —Micah Tyler

"Fight Song" —Rachel Platten

"Flowers" —Samantha Ebert

"Head Above Water" —Avril Lavigne

"My Jesus" —Anne Wilson

"Oceans (Where Feet May Fail)" —Hillsong United

"Raise a Hallelujah (Studio Version)" —Bethel Music

"Rise Up" —Andra Day

"Roar" —Katy Perry

"The Hurt & The Healer" —MercyMe

"These Days" —Jeremy Camp

"Who I Am" —Wyn Starks

"Yes I Will (Studio Version)" —Vertical Worship

"You Say" —Lauren Daigle

CHAPTER 1

The Awakening

I hear your cries. I have experienced them too. Today, heaven weeps with you. Today, the heavens open for you.

I know what it feels like to live under the weight of a dark cloud. It feels suffocating, like it is closing in on you.

This dark cloud may be chronic illness, a mental health battle, abuse, suicide ideation, or grief.

If you feel stuck in any of these, this book is for you. Let this book be a call to your heart to remind you who you are—that you are more than all of these things.

I can speak to all of them because I have not only survived them but used them to build the fire that God placed in my heart to write this book for you.

This book is close to a decade in the making, but really the last few years have been the refiner's fire. So many times, I have felt completely inadequate to write this book. That's the beauty of it: I had to lean into God and find the messages in my life *He* wanted me to share.

I actually started my book four years ago, and I have not used one word of *that* book. That book was all me, my processing. It was my schoolyard with God. I wrote *this* book, this entire book, in five days without burnout and without writer's block. I went to the mountains to commune with God. I left my family for a week and fasted from the world to hear these messages.

If God is not someone you have been able to sit with for some time, I understand. I have gone through my moments of unbelief and plain fury toward Him. I have cussed Him out in my prayers and felt like He abandoned me in my darkest moments.

I hope this book will introduce you to the God I have come to know in my life. Let these pages shine a light into your darkness. May you feel SEEN in your pain and heartache, but then may you be filled with HOPE for the life you are meant to be living. This book may activate you. This book may heal pieces you have felt were untouchable. This book just may change your life, if you let it.

I have written this entire book outside, grounded to the earth. All of it, except this chapter. The sky opened this morning and poured down on us. Upon waking, I heard that the angels were crying in honor of the work this week and for you.

This chapter I write from the cozy bed, listening to the rain hit the roof of the house and slide down the gutters. There is a fog that hugs the huge evergreen trees outside. Infuses them. Let this book hold you as that fog holds those trees. Let the essence of this book nourish the parts in you that are depleted.

My hope is that by the end of this book, you may have skills to challenge your beliefs about yourself and your body that you may feel is your prison. Let this book be a key to unlocking the chains that have been shackling you. You may not even realize you have them. Let these pages show you what is weighing you down, give you the clarity to name it, and give you the key to unlock it.

Even with the rain this morning I wanted to go write out on the covered front porch, for truly not one word had been written while I was inside the house. Then I heard "get back in bed." So I did. I sat here and felt that I needed to write to you from here because right now you are figuratively stuck in your house—the *house* of your worldview and the beliefs you hold about yourself. You don't even know what the yard of this house is. You can't see it because you are in your cozy bed. It is comfortable. It feels safe and warm, but really, that is the lie keeping you comfortably there: the lie of repeating to yourself, "I just need to get through this day." This lie, and others like it, hold you back from the life you were created to live. These lies keep you from being more. Remember, you are a spiritual being and this body is just a house. Your spirit wants more because it is bigger than all of this muck that has you trapped. Let go of the lies that have kept you trapped in this house and step into the life that you are capable of, a life of choice, agency, growth, and healing.

Please don't read this book and think these are just great stories and metaphors. Each has been prayed over for you and serves a purpose. I invite you to allow yourself to experience this book in your body. Allow it to shift and turn a tide in your heart. Let this be the beginning of your awakening.

CHAPTER 2

The Desire for More

I remember working out one morning with my three kids. They ranged in age from nearly one to three years old. My youngest was in the high chair eating breakfast, my oldest mimicking my every move with his own one-pound weights. My two-year-old was pushing a firetruck back and forth on the gray couch. I was jumping around the new display of scattered cars and trucks as I did the ski jump. *All I wanted was more.*

I wanted to be more than a mother, more than the dirty dishes and pile of dirty diapers. I wanted to be more than the magic boo-boo healer and more than the jungle gym for these boys. So, in my heart, I asked God to do more with my life. Make my life matter. Make my life impact someone else's for good. If there is one thing I have come to know it is if we sincerely ask God, He will answer, and so He did. Not in the way I would have thought. Not in the timeline I would have imagined and not as simply as the human side of me would have wanted, but my spirit within me sought it out. My inner self knew I was called to more and would not let my brain win. I am ever so grateful for that somewhat naïve version of myself that brought this massive crazy growth over the next nine years that has led me to writing for all of you.

Looking back, that moment was when I first began to realize the power I held inside of me by asking God for what I wanted. I began to witness a pattern in my life: when I was clear on what I was asking and then took it to God, He would answer. The more clear I was on what I wanted in my life, the more clearly I experienced God's answer. This was just the beginning of my awakening.

It may have been foggy, looking over the years, much like a construction site while it's being worked on seems like a disaster, but in the end a beautiful home is completed—one where lots of love and laughter are shared. It provides safety from the storms outside. There is warmth from a fire as the snow falls just past the window. The construction of my house I am sharing now was long and very messy. Sometimes I feel like I got off track from where God wanted me to go, and another storm would come through and knock down what I was building because I clearly asked that He build me to use for His glory, that I live a life to share a message that will make it so nobody could doubt in His goodness. And so it was. It had to be because I clearly asked for that miracle.

Now, I can see the completion of this beautiful house in sight. I can fully see the big picture, and I am so grateful for the refiner's fire that has developed me into the person I am now. For this version is a version that can help others.

Throughout this book I share some of the darkest moments of my life. In each of these experiences I have asked God what I could glean from the experience so that it was not experienced in vain. If you've experienced incredible heartache, abuse, sickness, or grief you may have found yourself asking:

Why me?

Why do bad things happen to good people?

What did I do to deserve this?

I don't claim to have the end-all be-all answers to these questions, but I can say I have spent many hours wrestling them, some in my youth and some in my adult years. In this book I share the perspective I have gained through my life experience, and maybe you'll find my answers can bring you peace of mind and stop the exhausting battle of needing to understand.

My ultimate prayer in writing this book is that you receive hope for your future and gain peace and healing from your past and the courage to step into choosing the life you want to create. You hold more power than you think you do. Do not fear this, use it to your advantage.

We often hold ourselves victim to our past. While I am not responsible for what happened in the story I share next, I no longer view myself as a victim to it, either. I have learned from the experience and am using it to help others and to become a better person, and it does not hold power over me anymore. As long as the experience held power over me, I was a victim to it. I took my power back the moment I chose to not let it take me down.

So what is it?

It was being raped.

If this is triggering, check in with yourself. I will not go into details. I simply share what I have learned from it and how I found healing. I hope you choose to read it so you can also benefit from what I have learned along the way.

CHAPTER 3

Rape

Time and time again in my life I heard that hard experiences were happening *for* me and not *to* me. I don't think that is true. Not everything I experience is for me, but *I* can use it and give it purpose.

I was just a teenager. Oh, I was so naïve, young, and prude. I knew about sex, I knew the functions, but I really didn't understand the body at all. It was a cold January and I was nearing my fifteenth birthday. I just remember the pain leading up to this experience. I had been feeling so heavy with emotions. I really needed a friend to talk to. This boy from my seminary class—a religious class I attended at high school— texted me. He was two years older, had a car, a job, and saw the perfect storm in me: a fatherless, lost, teenage girl wishing she had her father's love. He saw my brokenness and saw the right set of circumstances. I have no idea how premeditated this act was, or if he just seized the opportunity in the moment.

It was the evening of an emotionally hard day. I felt alone in this world, shut down and foggy in my mind. I had wanted to cry all day, but the tears would not come. Then I felt my phone buzz. I flipped my phone open and saw that he had texted. He wanted to swing by and talk. Since I really needed an ear, I asked my mother if we could just chat outside in his car. She agreed. We lived in an end townhouse unit. Next to our home was the common area between the houses and the road. A beautiful big tree had been growing for at least twenty years, and ducks often found refuge under it from the heat of the day. I used to find this little area so special. As he parked under this tree, I came out and slid into the front seat of his car. I remember I had an uneasy feeling. I thought it was just me feeling off. *It wasn't.*

That night I was raped, forced into the back seat, my life forever changed. I pleaded throughout the experience for it to stop. I called on God and pleaded that someone would walk past and interrupt this. *I don't care what it looks like, just make someone stop him.* I prayed my mother would just open the front door and yell out that I needed to come in, but she didn't. Why couldn't God stop this?

I was so embarrassed. Embarrassed by my body. I was so uncomfortable in my own skin. I was an awkward teenage girl in the thick of puberty and this was my first experience with anything sexual. I was so ashamed that my body had responded to his touch. I could have thrown up. How could my body lead him on like that? I felt betrayed by it. *How dare you, my body, betray me!* I swore it would never betray me again . . .

I don't know how it ended. I just remember sliding my hand on the carpet of the floor in the back seat and finding my phone and dashing out of there, not looking back. When I opened the door to go into my house, my mom was sitting in the family room. She was so annoyed that I had not been answering her texts to "come in the house now" and that she "wanted to go to bed." When I opened my phone, I had no messages from her. Not one. I wish she had just walked outside. I apologized and ran to my room. I shut my door, went to a corner of the bedroom, and cried. I cried for some time. Then I went to the shower and washed him off of me.

I went to school the next day and transferred out of his seminary class. I was not going to sit in a room with him again and be taught about God and "how we could be worthy Latter-day Saint members." I could not. Over the following few weeks, he must have told some of his friends about it because I had boys asking me for sex, too, *since I was now a slut* (according to them). I remember the first time I was called a slut in the school hallway. I ran to the bathroom and cried, shattered that my worth, dignity, and humanity had been stripped from me that night. Ultimately, these tauntings led me to transfer schools before the year was over.

So many times you hear, "Oh, this is happening *for* you."

I just want you to understand this: if you have been abused—mentally, physically, financially, spiritually, or sexually—it has NOT been "for you." It's happened. It sucks ass. It is NOT okay. It was not *for you*, **but that does not mean you can't give it purpose.**

Think of the experience as someone handing you logs. You can take those logs, haul them on your back, find an isolated place, and build four big walls around you. You can make the experience cut you off from others. Or, you can take those logs, build a fire, and let those logs give you purpose, direction, and burning in the bosom. Let that experience shape you into the strong, badass person you are. You may not be there now. You may have already built up the angry, thick walls around you, but you can knock them down. You can break those walls with a sledgehammer. Let out the anger you have contained. Let out the pain you have pushed down, and then set those logs on fire! Let them fuel your damn bonfire so the whole world is lit by your purpose. These experiences ultimately can break us, or they can build us into people who give others strength, who give others hope for tomorrow.

We have a choice.

We may not have had a choice in the experience, but we can use that experience for whatever purpose we want. Let it make you into the resilient person you are to become. Let it teach you empathy and how to hold space for others, and build a sixth sense of reading people who cross your path.

I know how hard it is to go through a trauma and feel so broken from it. I understand the pain, isolation, and questioning of "how could this happen to me?" For the first time, I struggled with my faith in God. Where was God in all of this?

"I didn't turn my back on you," He said.

I was so angry at God after my rape. I wondered, *"How could You do this to me? Have I not suffered enough abuse as it is?"*

I also radically struggled with my body not being my own anymore, not feeling safe anymore—like something had been stripped from me. This is when panic attacks became more rampant in my life. I had experienced anxiety before, but I had mostly battled depression the previous four years. After the rape, I started a deep fight with anxiety. I thought everyone was out to get me. I felt like everyone wanted to harm me. That simply wasn't the truth, but it became the truth I lived from and soon became the worldview I would have for the next fifteen years.

I confided in very few people those first few years after the trauma in the back seat of his sedan. One person I confided in was a school counselor, and it was about a year after I was raped. I was having a panic attack that took me out of class. My chest visibly moved up and down as I tried to steady my breath. My hands began to shake and I had totally dissociated from the lesson. I began to cry and excused myself from the classroom to go to the counselor's office. I was a real hot mess. As I sat in the counselor's room, she asked me what it was about. I confided in her about the betrayal I felt from my body during this act of being violated. I said that I feared that it meant I wanted it, that I was giving him permission, that it was consensual. What she said next was bold, hard to hear, and didn't feel helpful in the moment, but it was the beginning of my real healing.

She said, "Brooke, either you wanted it, gave him permission, and you are still pursuing guys, having sex, and are a whore . . . or you were violated, raped, and wrestle with it because you did not want it but your body responded as it would during a sexual act. That does not mean you agreed to it or that you wanted it. Just because your body responded, that does not mean you gave it the go. You are still a survivor of rape, even if your body was aroused."

I had never had anyone share this with me before. I had nobody I could ask and, as harsh and bold as it was at the moment, her words gave me permission to stop questioning if I was responsible for the act and to know I was not.

I was not.

You are not responsible for your rape. No matter how many times your attacker tries to blame you, no matter how many times you are shamed into thinking you did something to bring it on, only the attacker is responsible for not controlling themself. You can't control others and that is just the hard, ugly truth.

I held a grudge through all of this, toward God and myself. I was just honestly broken and had no safe place to go for healing.

CHAPTER 4

How Rape Affected My Marriage Bed

It would not be the last time I felt betrayed by my body. The next time would be in my marriage, when all of a sudden sex was okay and healthy and good, but to me it still wasn't. It was scary, painful, and bad. I had spent almost four years telling my body how bad it was for responding to being raped. I had spent all those days telling my body to shut down and not feel and that it had betrayed me. Now, all of a sudden, I wanted it to wake up with the snap of my fingers and work again. FEEL again. Holy shit, were my husband and I in for a ride!

My body did not just snap out of all the programming it had just spent years enduring. There were times that felt easier than others, moments of experiencing the light bulb—being aroused again and going, "This is how it is supposed to work." I spent so much time telling myself, *I am safe in my husband's arms,* but my nervous system insisted it knew better. It was stuck in the old loop, the old programming. The program of, "*This means danger! Shut down, dissociate, shut off.* Protect, protect, protect yourself!"

I married a saint. I honestly believe that. Trevor has held me tenderly in the middle of flashbacks, reminding me of where I really am, whom I am with, and that I am cherished and loved. His love and patience has played a big role in my healing those deepest wounds. What I didn't know was that in the process of him helping heal this part of me, I broke part of him. How do we fix it?

After each baby, I felt a little bit like I was back at square one. Having sex for the very first time after having a baby, I'd tense up—rigid, stiff, cold. He never rushed my healing. I know there were many times he felt frustrated, but he rolled with every tear and every pain and celebrated every breakthrough, every bit of healing, every tender experience together.

Slowly, over time, I reclaimed my body as mine through therapy, EMDR, workbooks, and personal development. All of it accumulated, healing me one crack at a time. The healing modality that was most effective for me was EMDR. I have not had another flashback since then and I did that work five years ago. That was honestly the time I reclaimed my power, took what was rightfully mine, and handled the situation the way I would have liked to back when the rape occurred.

Choosing to heal from this experience has been the most powerful thing for my marriage, and in the last five years we have grown closer in our intimacy. Allowing someone to truly know me in that way . . . it is the most amazing experience. He knows all of me. He watched and supported me through giving birth four times. He carried me to the bathroom when I was in paralysis. He has held my hair back when I've thrown up and cleaned up morning sickness. He has shown a selfless love I had never experienced in such pure form before, and through that I have found safety and confidence in my body. In our connection, I have found meaning.

I used to think I was just broken in the intimacy department, like I was ruined, couldn't be fixed. Sex was so physically painful for me for so many years of our marriage. I know that is bold to say, taboo to write, and might feel like an overshare, but women need to know that if they are experiencing that, they are not alone. Don't settle for the diagnosis of "painful sex." Yep, I was given that diagnosis when I went to the doctor after the birth of my first son. My son was close to a year old and still I could barely tolerate the act of lovemaking. The doctor told me that was just the way it was going to be.

I spent many years working through emotional healing, physical healing, and ultimately finding out more diagnoses that helped heal this part of me. Sex is sacred, magical, beautiful. Don't give up hope on it being all of that for you too. If you are not experiencing that yet, don't give up. Don't accept no as an answer, or pain as the diagnosis—because it absolutely isn't one. Don't settle for anything less than healing and the belief that it is possible. I'm not a unicorn. It is not just possible for me. In fact, because I have healed, that's proof that it is possible for everyone!

Even though I was the one who went through the horror of being raped, I wasn't the only one affected. Trevor had his own battle and journey to walk as my partner, my husband, my friend, and the one I share my bed with.

I believe it is essential to understand and hear both sides for the healing to be long-lasting, so I have asked him to share his perspective and his side of the story. He shares his experience as the one to hold me as I emotionally and physically traveled back in time to a place I was victimized, how it was to hold me through the years of healing and the repercussions of the rape I endured.

CHAPTER 5

How My Rape Affected My Husband

I knew being raped would affect me. I had no idea how much it would end up affecting my marriage. Maybe I was naïve, or perhaps I just could not understand that rape had not only been a generational trauma inflicted on me but it was rewriting the cellular code in my body.

I'm ever so grateful Trevor was willing to go deep here with me and share his side of the experience. Entering our marriage, if we had been able to be more prepared about the fallout the rape would have, that could have collapsed time on our healing process. Writing this section together has been a big part of healing at a cellular level where I was not aware was still broken.

I was reminded that with every growth we experience, we have to be willing to go deeper with healing in areas of our lives that before we were not able to go deep enough to heal. Trevor and I, individually and as a couple, are now people who are able to sit in the discomfort, sit in the conversations without hiding or withdrawing, to heal the deepest parts of this wound. Together, we are setting our marriage free and breaking the generational trauma.

What I wish I would have understood is that I was not the only one who would need healing from this.

Trevor healed me through corrective sexual experiences. I believe that the only way to fully heal from sexual trauma is to have corrective experiences. He was willing to hold that space with me for years, patiently, lovingly, gently healing each broken part of me. In the process of him healing me, I did not see that in return he would have wounds that needed healing. That has been part two of our journey.

I see this clearly as I read the words he wrote, the pain it caused him at a personal level. This part has to be spoken about, has to be brought out of the shadows so marriages can experience full unity, healing, and joy in intimacy.

In Trevor's words:

I have an internal battle going on inside on how real and open to be here. Could this help others? Brooke sure thinks it will. But what is the cost to me? Do I really want to let people in? I really don't. This isn't for you. This is mine. I feel that I am inviting the world into my bed.

People I know will read this. Will they think I am strong and courageous? Probably. Does that mean I want to let you in? Nope.

What am I supposed to say? Saying nothing seems so much easier and incredibly less vulnerable. What can I say that doesn't sound incredibly selfish? Because that's how I feel. Selfish. Who cares what I want?

Expectations? Unmet expectations? What were those expectations? There seem to be more questions than any words of wisdom to be shared here. But maybe questions are what is needed.

"Rape" was just a word, a thing that happens to other people far away, never to those whom I know and those around me.

How naïve was I?

There are other stories of those in my life who experienced rape, but those stories aren't mine to tell. Did those experiences of others affect my life? Absolutely.

Let me back up and share a little of my own trauma, a religious trauma. What's up with this shit religious upbringing? A woman was "the prize" and what an awesome prize to have. I always felt "less than" women. The Church made sure to reiterate this every six months in a general men's meeting (broadcast around the world), where men were chastised for being prone to pornography addiction and not prone to treating women right. Women were placed on a pedestal. Chosen over men. I felt like they were chosen over me. How lucky would I be to have one choose me? But would that even happen? After all, I didn't hold a worthless title, such as "return missionary," in the Church—a title that was so important in my religious world. But I chose to not have the title, so I did it to myself. Right?

Well, luckily for me, I found someone who didn't need me to have that title. I got "the prize." When Brooke said "yes" to marrying me, I knew I had "won." She's the best person I've ever known, and she chose me as emphatically as I chose her.

We all have expectations. Expectations in life, work, play, church, marriage. But what are the expectations in a marriage? Can I put them into words? Do I even consciously know what these expectations are that I have? Am I meant to know them? Am I asking too many questions?

I absolutely thought things were going to go differently. Naïve again? Maybe. How was I to know how the rape of my prize would affect our marriage? *Affect me?*

Our bed. . . yup, things did not go the way I thought they would. Unmet expectations? Yup. But what are these expectations?! I remember having thoughts like, *How can you not feel safe with me? How can you be triggered? I didn't do anything to harm you. I'm the safe place. I'm the calm in the storm. I'm your rock. Why is this happening? Why am I dealing with your flashbacks in the middle of our time? Why does this get to have so much power over us?* Seems pretty selfish, huh?

How do you deal with all of that?

What I really wanted was for Brooke to *feel* how I love her, treasure her, cherish her. How I want to keep her safe, to help her feel whole. But I wasn't able to make that happen. This felt like pure failure.

I kept wondering, *is this me*? Sure feels like it. I'm for sure not a winner there.

I didn't want to deal with it. It felt so much easier to distance myself. I remember thinking, "If I'm not present, then it can't affect me. *Right?"* To be distant, does that mean to be *physically* away? I wish. It would probably be easier. But no, emotionally distant, distant in connection, distant in vulnerability—just distant.

I realized that If I didn't have expectations then there wouldn't be disappointment there. Protection for me?

Yup!

Sign me up! So, I decided to drop the expectations.

Who needs to be intimate? Not me. I can tell that to myself over and over. *Ya, I'll do that.*

Not tonight? *Sounds good.* It's been awhile? *Oh well.*

I don't feel desired? I can't fail if I'm not desired. *Another flashback?* It's okay. No needs here . . .

But what about needs . . . a man has "needs." What the hell is that? Needs? Sexual needs? Who are you to impose on me what I need because of my gender? You don't know me. Just because society says this is how something is, that doesn't mean that's how it actually is. To hell with you and your societal norms!

What is a need? Do we all have needs? Needs are something you can't go without and still survive. You NEED food. You NEED water. You NEED air. But you sure as shit don't NEED sex. You may have desires, but that isn't for the survival of a single human being. Creation and furthering the human race? Yes, but you won't physically die if you don't have sex.

Expectations and distance. Drop one and embrace the other. That's safe. Right? What's the cost in doing that? I'm not sure. But maybe I can share a little of what the cost has *felt like* for me.

Dropping expectations feels like repeating a lie so many times that my mind starts to believe it, but my body and soul feel betrayed by it. Maybe the lie you tell yourself is, "I don't want sex. It's fine. I don't feel rejected." And the truth that helps you feed that lie is, "she isn't rejecting *me*. She's rejecting *sex*." That part is true. What isn't true is your belief that you *don't* feel that rejection in your bones and internalize it to be a rejection of *you*.

Then, to avoid this internalized feeling of rejection, maybe you distance yourself emotionally from your partner to ease the *pain of rejection*. "If

I believe I don't *desire* sex with my partner, then I won't pursue that intimacy with my partner, and I won't risk internalizing her triggers, anxiety, or tension as a rejection of *me*." Lower expectations, more distance, less emotional safety for both of us.

Have I handled the rape of my prize correctly? **Probably not.**

Have I failed? **Yup.**

Have we worked our asses off together? **Yes.**

Have we worked on healing? **Yes.**

Do we have power over that selfish act from so many years ago that has affected us? **I would like to think so.**

Are things perfect? **No.**

Are things where I want them to be? **I'll be bold and say no.**

Are we on a growing path? **Yes.**

Have there been huge strides? **Yes.**

So, where has God been in all of this? He's been there every step of the way. Have I leaned on Him? I wish I could say yes. My pride said I could do it. But I'm tired. Tired of the helping. Tired of being the safe spot. Tired of being strong. Tired of the walls. Tired of being distant. If only I would have utilized God, could I have helped better? Sooner? Safer?

I feel that I have been good at playing the cards that I/we have been dealt. Has life looked like I expected? No?

Has life and marriage with Brooke been worth it? **That is a YES.**

Rape is something that affects both partners, which isn't something I ever comprehended until it was at my doorstep. It has been our deepest challenge to overcome in our marriage . . . but it has pulled us together in ways that nothing else has ever done. I have watched Brooke rise over again and again. And I have risen with her.

Marriage is not what we expect it to be.

But it is in the darkest times that we find the love we were looking for. Rising together has been a beautiful gift.

CHAPTER 6

Transitioning Faith

I was barefoot on the cold tile floor in the bathroom. It felt icy smooth beneath my feet and as I walked into the bathroom to brush my teeth one night, I stopped dead in my steps. I was staring at the tub but did not see it. All I could think was, *if Jesus walked into the room, I wouldn't know Him.* I would not KNOW Him. I know *of* Him. I know the stories of His life, but I do not have a relationship with Him as I always wanted. It was at that moment I knew something had to change. I had no idea what, though. I grew up praying, reading scriptures daily, memorizing the verses. I was, by all definitions, a "Molly Mormon." If you do not know what that means, it is only a term to say I tried to follow every LDS doctrine to the letter, and still I found myself not knowing Him. I pushed this thought out of my mind, comforted myself with my standing record of checklists, and concluded I was judging myself too harshly. My third baby, after all, was only two weeks old and my oldest would be turning three at the end of the week. Now was not the time to have a faith crisis. Or so I thought.

Since when does God believe in a human's perspective of perfect timing? In fact, that is what makes God's sense of humor so humorous. It does not line up with our perfect timing. His timing is always far more perfect than our human minds can comprehend. This thought was just a warming plate thrown to my heart to prepare me for the weekend to come. When my faith was challenged, my heart became open and the rose-colored glasses I had been wearing were shattered—all in one rainy afternoon. The rain felt poetically appropriate for the tears I cried that day. The angels were shedding tears with me. It felt like all the weight of what I was going through—my worldview—was collapsing in on itself and I had to stay open to what God was presenting me with, trusting that the truth would set me free. I was still completely unaware of the chains I had been carrying through life like a badge of honor. God was calling me to lay them down. This is the story of how He broke through my thick, protective walls.

Losing the religion of my childhood felt like a loss of a person, like someone near and dear to me—like a mom or a dad—had died. The pain was two layers deep because it was not just a loss of religion but also the resulting loss of all contact with extended family after this loved one's death. That extended family was my church community, my "ward family," and they were now gone as well.

It seemed that somehow my faith crisis was contagious. It was as though my doubt would spread. Since I no longer believed, if they got too close to me, all of a sudden they magically might not believe either.

It's reminiscent of cooties from the playground. What are we, third graders? Can we not have adult conversations about people's beliefs anymore? It's as if two humans cannot have differing religious beliefs. I felt as though people thought, *if you don't think the way I think, I can't be around you.* The loss of community was shocking to me because Trevor and I were never questioning the LDS Church, and we weren't *looking* to leave.

The name of this book actually comes from the following experience.

Trevor's mother had a very small kitchen fire. My husband wanted pictures because he used to be a fireman, but she wouldn't send any pictures. My mother-in-law didn't want any evidence of the fire because she was a renter. The silly thing is that she had overcooked something in a pan and it got really smokey in the kitchen. There had never been a real fire; it was just soot on the white cabinets. We walked into her house and I handed her my three-week-old baby. I had three under three. As we filed into the home, Trevor, who was a realtor, said that he noticed the house across the street was up for sale. Then he asked his mother why she hadn't told the neighbors her son was a realtor. Without thinking she blurted out, "I haven't gone to church in four months."

This was earth-shattering news to us. My mother-in-law was such a devout Mormon that she'd spend Halloween in the temple. When we were getting married, she told us that since we were getting married in the temple, our marriage was "real." Marriages outside of the temple were not "real" in her eyes. She said they were just playing house. So, you can see why her response was so surprising to us!

Trevor asked her, "Why haven't you been going to church?" She deflected his questions and responded, "Oh, how about when you put the kids to bed tonight, I'll come to your house." He was not having that.

He sat down at her kitchen table with her laptop and her Mormon scriptures, and I started cleaning the soot off her white cabinets. As he asked her questions, she would give a reason she didn't believe anymore and he would look it up and say, "Oh, yeah, that doctrine doesn't line up. That makes sense." I was looking at him across the room and panicking, worrying that my husband was going to leave the Church—the church we were so devout to, the church we were raising our three boys in. All I could think was, "How am I to raise three worthy priesthood holders without my husband believing in the same faith? What am I going to do?" I was dead set on not listening to this conversation. I kept saying to myself over and over, "This conversation will *not* rock my faith. I know God is real."

About two hours into this conversation, I could see Trevor was really out the door. He no longer believed in the LDS religion. I said to God, "Okay, God, if the LDS Church is actually true, it can withstand these questions" because that made sense to me. And so, I started to actively listen to the next part of the conversation.

After three hours of deep religious conversation with my husband and mother-in-law, my mind was exhausted. I asked my mother-in-law to invite over a Christian woman because I had questions I wanted to ask someone who was raised as a Christian. She called over someone I had met previously, but I had no idea the woman's husband was a pastor. They both came over to my mother-in-law's house, and we began another three-hour conversation.

As we sat together at the kitchen table, we compared Mormon doctrine with biblical Christian doctrine. During that conversation, I discovered that my beliefs align more closely with biblical Christianity than with Mormonism. *How could that be?* I was raised Mormon. Somehow, my view of God was Christian, *not Mormon*.

I knew that Mormons taught that you could become Gods. I did not realize they taught that their God was once a man that had become God and *that* is the God they worshipped. That is not my God. No, no. Ultimately, when people ask me why I left the LDS Church, it comes down to the simple answer: I cannot worship a God I do not believe in. I simply cannot pray to a God who was once a man; my God is so much bigger than that. My God is so much more beyond that. The Mormon belief is us trying to put God into a box that our human brains can understand. I don't want to worship a God I can understand. If I can understand Him, then I could do it on my own. I need the God who is the Almighty, the One and Only, the One Who Knows All. I need *that* God to get me through my shit. So ultimately, my one-line answer is, "I couldn't pray to that God because He is not mine."

That night my life changed, all because of a small kitchen fire and hours around the table.

I had no idea that walking away from my religion meant walking away from community and family. I mean, I knew it to a degree, but I think I was still shocked when I experienced the shunning and ignoring. I was so shocked that people just stopped talking to me. It felt as though talking about the biblical Jesus would somehow condemn their kids to hell. And even worse, it seemed as if I were contagious. It was like giving them a different perspective on Jesus's love was dangerous, or that I couldn't respect their boundaries and not talk about something they don't believe in in front of their kids. I wanted to say to them, "I'm a mother. I respect your boundaries." This experience was absurd and filled with loneliness.

I think one of our greatest gifts in our faith transition was allowing ourselves to take it at our own pace. My husband was a born-again Christian in under three hours. It took me ten days, which is still very very fast, but those ten days felt like a lifetime. During those ten days, seeing my husband so far ahead of me in his understanding and grasp of our situation left me feeling a heavy responsibility. I was faced with the daunting task of taking our three children out of a religion that I had always been told was the only way to God. It's not just my life, it's theirs, and it's their childhood in Utah. It's their friendships. It's their dating lives. But I had to lay that all down at the cross.

Before I told my family that I left the LDS Church, I spent many months processing and making sure that I didn't have any anger left in my grieving. I wanted to come from a place of peace. I wanted to be so clear that I knew who I was and where I was at. As I began to share my new beliefs with friends, I was so surprised. I found that some people were so grateful I believed in God while other people would say to me, "You realize not all churches believe in the same God, right?" I would respond, "Yes, that is why I'm leaving!" I had no idea how much it was going to shift and change my relationships, and that is scary! The fear of sharing almost held me stagnant, stuck in religion. Ultimately, one afternoon while I was driving home, I heard on the radio a verse about choosing God over other relationships, over convenience. I knew at that moment that I was making the right choice, and that gave me the strength to finally tell my family.

There is no right time to break it to your mother that you are the black sheep of the family. Prior to our conversation, I'm not sure if she had any idea that I had left the religion of my childhood. I told her I had spent the previous five months unpacking my beliefs. I know it was quite unexpected for her. She responded with shock, love, and wanting to make sure I knew what I was really walking away from. What she couldn't see was what I was walking *toward*: not a religion but a relationship with Jesus.

I wanted to make sure when it came time to sharing with the rest of my family about my transition in faith that I had already grieved and processed and knew where my heart stood on religion versus a relationship with God. This was important to me because I did not want my family to feel defensive of their beliefs based on my emotional state. I wanted the conversations to be healthy and overall positive. I knew I could not control their emotional reactions, and I had to be prepared to give them space to process and ask whatever questions they had. I won't speak for any of my family members on how they received the news. I will just share what my experience was.

I made phone calls one by one to each of my siblings, telling them the news the same evening I had told my mother, as she requested. It was like ripping a Band-Aid off. It felt overwhelming to make all those calls in one day. Some conversations were rather short, others seemed heavy and held a lot of shock and emotions.

I watched my language as I told my siblings the news, only sharing my experience and my perspective. I told them I had compiled doctrinal reasons using only Latter-day-Saint approved reading topics if they wanted to understand why I was making such a radical shift in my life. Ultimately, none of them ever wanted to see it and I just ended up publishing it as a blog.

Most of my family had very few questions about my leaving. Most of them used phrases like, "I don't want to know why you left," or, "Was it over doctrine, or was it over something that happened at church?" Most of my family was just grateful I still have faith in God, which I understand, but I also found it shocking that they were okay with me *just* having faith in God.

You may relate to this experience with religion, or maybe there's another area of your life that you've been feeling called to change and you don't want to listen because of the cost. This is a call to follow your knowing, to live fully no matter the cost, no matter the fallout! The cost feels so great right now, but it's so much sweeter on the other side. I may have lost friendships, community, and even family, but what I received has brought so much joy that surpasses the losses.

The cost was great but the reward is I now know God in a way I never could have within the confines of religion. I have a new community that is so willing to serve with loving, open arms, to be Jesus's hands and feet in my life. I have new friends that have become family. Whatever the potential cost that is keeping you stuck, know that the sacrifice brings the sweetness on the other side. I could not have imagined all the rewards on this side of following my inner knowing, being called out of the dominant religion of my geographical area and my childhood. I wasn't searching. God literally just ripped the blinders off my eyes and I couldn't unsee what I saw. Once I couldn't unsee it, staying would have caused me suffering, illness, and being stuck.

Your transition in your life may not be religion. You may relate it to another calling that you are hearing and ignoring. Know in your being that God is calling you to something greater, sweeter, more miraculous than you could ever know. Trust in yourself. Trust in living a fuller life, a more fulfilled life, and that by doing so you are giving people around you permission to do the same.

CHAPTER 7

Who is God?

Our human minds cannot compute what our spiritual being can experience. This body contains the spirit to *this* realm. Gravity can affect water to create a beautiful waterfall. The two working together is what makes a waterfall majestic, a creation that we seek out and love to experience. Think of the body and the spirit as a team like gravity and water creating a waterfall. Together, the body and spirit make this life a beautiful, majestic experience we seek out.

If you were raised in a religion like mine, you may think of God as a father figure. This is the only way our minds can make sense of such a being. The problem with this is that we then take our earthly experiences with a father figure, or a religious figure like a pastor, bishop, or prophet, and then we project that onto who God is. These men often have hurt us in deeply unforgettable ways. Please do not judge God based on these men. So many people struggle with God because they have a painful relationship with their father.

Religion is what man created. Relationships are what God created. God is love. Jesus didn't come to earth to give us impossible standards and make us feel awful for never living up to them. He came to break that. All the rules of the Old Testament were there to remind us we could never be perfect. We could never earn our way to heaven. We needed someone who was without fault to pay that price. **That is Love.**

Do you question if there is a God? If so, you may know Him as some judge in the sky who is waiting to point out all you've done wrong here on earth. You may relate Him to a parent that you could never please or do anything right for. This is the human mind trying to understand a deity that cannot fit into the human box. The brain is trying to make sense of something it simply cannot. God is an eternal being. He **is** love. When you experience true, unconditional love from someone who serves out of genuine care rather than obligation, you experience pieces of heaven on earth.

I once had a pastor explain it to me like this: if I'm a stick figure on a piece of paper and God is a rubix cube then I, a two-dimensional being, cannot understand the cube. To me, He is only a square. Therefore, I cannot fully understand who He is.

Being able to release myself from needing to fully understand God has freed me of believing He is a judge in the sky and let me be open to getting to know God as He says He is to me. I let go of experiencing God with my mind and began to experience God with my spirit.

I love leaning into God spirit to spirit. It releases my mind from the need to fully understand. I know what I write now is reflective of my current relationship with God. What I write about Him in five years will reflect how our relationship has grown. I release pressure of what it looks like. I speak what He asks me to speak, share the miracles He works in my life, and let go of the rest.

It is not my job to convince you He is a real, loving figure who wants the best for you. I am just sharing whom I experience Him to be in my life. My only prayer through writing this is that you may be willing to open your mind and heart with curiosity to explore your relationship with God. Let Him show you who He is. Ask and He will answer.

The mind loops, like a record jumping back to the beginning because of a scratch. God does not loop for me. He shares His message directly, quickly, and if I missed the memo, dismissed it as my own thought, and it has to be reshown, it usually is shown to me in a new way the next time. A theme will appear of letting this be easy—holding onto faith or letting go of suffering, for example—but the message will never be received the same way twice. When something is coming from me, it is just like a broken record saying the same thing over and over again.

Another way to discern if it is from God is that if you do not write it down or share it with someone to bring it to this world, you will forget. I had a mentor share this with me, and just to test the point, I once "forgot" to write the message down to refer back to. I did forget it! I will never make that mistake again! God's messages are too important. God's messages to you are your private scriptures for your life. Don't downplay what He says. Own the words.

Like any muscle, this relationship, when you spend time building it, will grow. Let God show you who He is and that He is real. Approach with curiosity, and let go of the old beliefs you may be carrying from others or childhood religion. I know God will show up for you as He has for me. All you must do is ask, listen, and receive!

Do you have a bold ask? I used to barter with God, like if I do this for you, will you do this in return? It's silly because I could never do anything worthy of Him. That's why we need Jesus. Yet, God humored me, met me where I was, and always came through. Not because of my work but because of who He is.

I'm bold now. I've grown in my relationship with God. I know I can't *earn* His favor. Instead, I say, "I will do whatever you tell me to do." That's how this book came to be. Have you ever boldly, bravely, in complete faith asked God to show you what is next for you? What's the most important thing for me to do today? What business am I to build? What do I write in this social media post? What are you calling me to create?

Your life changes, molds, shapes, and heals you when you live in the daily ask of God. It can be as simple as, "What is the most important thing for me to do today?" or as bold as, "Lead me to create with you a program to change the world. Provide healing and growth and open the heavens."

I challenge you to add this to your routine. End your day asking about tomorrow. Ask for clarity and guidance. Then, open your day with God and ask again. Ask for Him to show you, tell you, the most important message or thing for you to do that day.

Don't worry if it's hard to hear at first. It takes time and practice to drop into your spirit heart to hear God. Within a few days it will become easier, and slowly you will lean on this muscle to do all your business and life with God. Who said we had to wait to die to live in the presence of the Divine? Why can earth not be a personal heaven where we communicate with the Divine each and every day? I challenge you who are not sure if you believe in God to ask Him to show you He is real. HE will show up for you as He has for me.

CHAPTER 8

The Dark Side of Motherhood

Moms, I'm speaking directly to you right now. While this message can apply to anyone, in this chapter, I'm focusing on mothers.

Don't let the world take you down.

Don't let belief of what motherhood *should* look like drown out the whispers of whom your heart is calling you to be.

I almost didn't listen and it nearly killed me. **I was called to be more, and I am done hiding.**

As mothers, we are constantly seeking. Seeking to do things right, to be seen, to be appreciated, to not mess up our kids. It is not wrong to want to be the best mother, but it is wrong to let it consume you until you are a shell of a person. **You are more than a mother.** You're not going to ruin your kids by following the call of your heart, but **you are going to mess them up because you're human.**

You cannot mess your kids up past God's healing. *Take comfort in that.* And allow yourself to be MORE.

I told myself to play small. I hid my gifts. **And it broke me.**

When I first shared that I had postpartum psychosis, I thought it would never leave my therapist's office. I thought I would never break through the shame I felt from it. Psychosis isn't just depression and anxiety—it's full-on hallucinations; it is thoughts that your precious baby should no longer be living and neither should you. It is wrestling literally with the devil, and guess what?

God won.

God fucking won.

I am alive to write you this book . . . and that is proof.

Writing this book is so much more than words on a page. This is breaking through any self-doubt, shame, or cobwebs I still have so that I can fully accept and love myself. Writing this book ensures that my confidence is internal, that my love is from the only source that matters, and I can share the message I am called to write regardless of how it is received. I believe there is no dollar amount you can put on that type of self-acceptance.

But leading up to that triumph of self-worth is a maze of darkness that I know well.

This darkness . . . *it doesn't define you.*

I know how insane it feels when you are stuck in depression.

I know the darkness of psychosis.

I know you're shut down . . . and I am here.

It feels hopeless. I know you wonder . . . is healing even worth it?

I know you might hate life so much right now. I understand that the mountain feels impossible to climb, the air is thin, and the terrain is rocky.

I know that you might literally think you are crazy, and you are scared of your own thoughts. You can't sleep at night because of your nightmares, and you wonder, "Are they dreams or are they reality?"

I remember my nightmares escalating so high I had to be put on nightmare medication. I had lost all touch with reality. I didn't know what was false and what was true. The illusions of my mind created a reality that I no longer could live in.

This is the dark side of motherhood that no one talks about.

And it ends now!

You are not alone if you have asked yourself these questions . . .

> *Could I actually harm my perfect baby?*
>
> *Why won't he stop crying?*

Can I really do this?

If I fall asleep, will a nightmare wake me?

Will I wake in a sweat, check that all are okay, and then have my mind race the rest of the night?

I prayed for the morning sun and as soon as it rose, I dreaded getting up again.

I would pray the following night would come quickly and that it would finally include rest. Then night would fall and somehow I would be back in this crazy cycle of fearing sleep, and no rest would come.

I wanted to be anywhere, anywhere BUT here. Like spiders were crawling on my skin, the need to jump right out of my body seemed to be the only option to stop the noise.

I swore people could see how crazy I felt. I was certain everyone must know what a horrible mother I was. I was so surprised to discover that people thought I had it all together during this time, and I was drowning.

Wait . . . drowning doesn't even begin to describe it. But, how was I to save myself from drowning and keep my baby above water at the same time?

I know what it is like to fall instantly in love with your baby after birth, and to not. I know what it is like to truly believe you don't even love your baby, but you would die to protect him, yet you resent him for triggering it all. I know the pain of loss—the pain of losing a baby you wanted so badly, and the pain of losing a baby you didn't want at all. I thought I must be broken. *Surely, no good mom would ever feel this way.*

There is a hole in your gut and all you can think about is that this hole is so painful. It is deeply distracting. The all-encompassing pain makes it physically hard to breathe.

It hurt to breathe everyday.

It was like I had to remind myself about this bodily function that would normally work on its own.

Just the act of *thinking* of breathing sucked so much life out of me.

How was I supposed to heal psychosis when I had to think about putting one foot in front of the other just to get out of bed?

On top of raising four children who relied on me for every aspect of their life!

Then I had to think about the act of breathing?

Psychosis felt like a slime I couldn't wash off my body. No matter how hard I tried and no matter the soap or even chemicals I used, I couldn't get rid of it. I couldn't hide from it; it just clung to me like a parasite. It felt as if I were rolling in a mud pile like a pig that *wanted* to be stuck there. I was fighting with the devil but he was more than on me—he was in my head. I couldn't discern my thoughts from him, what I was seeing from what he was putting there. Was there really a guy after me, or was I just running like a crazy person down the road?

Was I really crazy?

I think I'm crazy, and what do they do with the mom that's crazy?

What are they going to do to my children?

What if they don't let me back?

What if I'm an unfit mother?

What is the government going to do to them?

I felt like I'd protect them with my life *and* I also hated them with my entire being. I got out of bed every day because I had to for them *and* I resented them with everything in me for making me get out of bed. I was so bitter and angry. I hated motherhood. I was lost in motherhood *and* I thought motherhood was going to fix me. I thought motherhood would be magical and healing and everything they promised me when I was a teenager—**and it was a lie.**

I felt so blindsided.

Why did they lie to me?

How do people want this?

How do they willingly do this?

If I could have turned back time, I would have. Like Dorothy clicking her red heels, I would have gone back.

Luckily, that's not how my story ended.

I didn't listen to the demons in my head. **And I praise God that I didn't.**

I want to remind you . . . *you* are more than a mother and there's healing, there's hope, and there's identity outside of motherhood. When I was able to separate Brooke from motherhood, that is when I began to heal. When I look at motherhood as something I am able to *do* and not *all* that *I am*, the equation changes. I am more than a mother, and so are you. If you haven't experienced depression or anxiety after having a baby, that is amazing and I honor you. Don't think that you are less of a mother because you haven't struggled.

Motherhood is not a competition. **Your hard is just different than my hard.**

I see you.

I know the loneliness, the questioning—am I doing this right?—and then looking to others for answers, and just hoping that the next book you pick up will be the manual the baby was supposed to be sent with, *but it won't be*. There's nothing wrong with looking to others for guidance, for help. Heck, *I'm writing a book!* But the truth is, the answers you need for *your* child are within you. The guidance you need for your baby is that *gut instinct* everyone is telling you to push down and override when your baby's screaming and they tell you to set a timer, but your gut is screaming, clawing at the chalkboard, "pick up your baby!"

That's the manual.

Lean in and listen to it.

Don't let others tell you you're crazy for honoring the mother within you. Remember that she's just *a part of you,* within you. She's not the entirety of who you are. You are a human outside of being a mother and **your needs**—*they matter.* I wish someone had told me after I had my first son that my needs still mattered. I wish someone had told me to take care of myself and not just "sleep when they sleep." That wasn't helpful. But I wish someone had actually told me to soak in the tub, and lean into a good book, and find a friend at a coffee shop to connect with.

When our needs are ignored by our own selves, we become easily depleted and more brittle. I had abandoned all of my needs. I had four kids under the age of five. *My body had birthed* four kids in five years. I hadn't slept in five years. My basic needs were depleted. **This was a code-red situation.**

I remember distinctly that the screaming wouldn't stop and I was too scared to wake up my husband and tell him that I really just wanted to shake the screaming out of the baby.

Mom, those thoughts are common, and they don't make you a horrible mother. You are human, and it's okay to put your baby down and take a deep breath. It's okay to ask for help. It's okay to admit when you're at your breaking point.

But then listen to your instincts and know when to walk back in and pick up your baby and soothe them. And just like you walk back in and show up for that baby, **show up for yourself** because you are just like that infant crying in the crib who has needs that need to be met. You put the timer on yourself and say, "In ten minutes, if the screaming (you being at your wits end) is still going on, then I'll check it out."

But if you never check in on yourself and you learn to function while the siren is going, pretty soon you no longer hear the siren and it becomes your new functioning level. You must learn to care for yourself when this siren first goes off. Set the timer and give yourself what you need for ten minutes. One ten-minute break won't fix anything, but taking care of you in ten-minute increments multiple times throughout the day is equivalent to a pilot adjusting their plane's flight pattern one degree. At first, it won't seem to change the direction much, but in time, that one degree will take that flight to a completely different destination. So, too, can caring for yourself in short increments change the course of your motherhood journey.

Many mothers believe they're good mothers if their babies meet milestones, are healthy, sleep through the night, nurse easily, smile, and don't cry. Trying to live up to these unrealistic expectations we put on ourselves is what creates the crazy inside of us. The pressure to reach the unattainable creates insanity. We juggle motherhood and often neglect self-care activities that remind us we are also humans with basic needs that deserve to be met.

I know that this role of motherhood is very isolating and many do not speak of these topics. It is my prayer that through the sharing of my life, I can save many mothers from death: death of self, death of dreams, death of physical body. Protect them from the demons that know the mother is a powerful person in a home.

If you have forgotten the power you wield as a mother, if you ignore the haunting voices in your mind and stuff down the crazy that wreaks havoc on the body, it is just like a fire. And if you just choose to ignore a fire, it will grow until the flames are out of control and there is no saving the house.

And that is how I ended up in the mental hospital.

CHAPTER 9

Mental Hospital

I thought I'd go to the hospital and get fixed . . . get better and then we would never speak of it again. I was never going to tell anyone.

I sat on the edge of my bed. My back was to the door that was open at all times. I had been sobbing for the last twenty-four hours, regretting every decision that had led to me willingly walking into the hospital. I was pleading with God, "Please let me out. I promise I won't kill myself. Just let me out."

My red, puffy eyes were closed from crying so hard when I swore I felt the bed move beside me. I opened my eyes and nobody was there, *but Jesus was.* I know He was. I closed my eyes again and I could just see Him beside me. He said, "This experience isn't just for you. *It is for others too.*" He told me that this experience was meant to save others, that I would go on to make waves in our mental healthcare system for moms. I saw myself talking on stage, in rooms one-on-one, in office buildings, and in meetings. God was gracious enough to give me a glimpse of the future, enough to keep me fighting because if I was not enough to fight for, *you were.*

My therapist once told me that on the day she met me she knew I would survive because I said I had to fix the system. She saw in me the fire to help others, even when I couldn't see my own brokenness. She recognized that my drive wasn't just for myself; I had a purpose, even at my breaking point, and purpose keeps us going.

To this day, I struggle with my hospital stay. I know it happened as it needed to, but sometimes I wonder if I could have managed without it. Then I remember it wasn't just about me, and I find peace with it again.

Safety is what I was always seeking. When I couldn't find it within me, I was lucky to experience it in my marriage.

Trevor is my person, my safe place, the calm to my chaos. He was the only reason I was still breathing when I walked into that hospital, not only because he had been babysitting my every move but because God used my love for Trevor in the most natural, selfish, human way to keep me breathing. I literally couldn't handle the idea of him loving someone else the way he loves me, *the way I love him.* Our connection is unique. I know everyone says that about their person, but when I say it, I really mean it. I did not trust easily or naturally. God just gave me instant trust in this man.

MENTAL HOSPITAL

God used this very human side of me to keep me going. The jealousy I felt thinking of him remarrying—which he might need to do more out of necessity than anything else—had me so furious that I would take another step forward each day. That crazy love for him ultimately led me to willingly walk into the mental hospital. I couldn't bear the thought of him feeling responsible for my death. Like if he had watched me more closely, or not fallen asleep, maybe I'd still be here. The guilt of him being the one to find me dead haunted me. I saw this play out in my mind multiple times: my spirit would hang around waiting for him to find me, and I would see his reaction. So I couldn't follow through with killing myself. My love for Trevor was the reason I walked into the mental hospital, hand-in-hand with him. He was my "why" when I first walked in there.

I knew I had postpartum psychosis. But the lady checking me in got stuck on bipolar disorder because her son had bipolar disorder, and that really planted the belief in the doctor's mind that I was just a bipolar mom not on medication and trying to deny her diagnosis. I was deemed paranoid and considered defiant when I tried to advocate for what I needed from the staff therapist and psychiatrist. I knew they weren't going to take me seriously, and ultimately I would have to play their game to be released.

They originally wanted to hold me for at least ten days. The problem was, I was uninsured. My doctor spent three hours calling hospitals the day I was admitted, trying to A) find an available bed, and B) find one willing to take me uninsured. Can you believe my life meant less because I'd be on a payment plan to pay for this stay? It really angers me that the value of a mother's life comes down to the insurance card she does or doesn't hold. I am very grateful for a family doctor who works outside the confines of insurance and saw value in my life outside of a dollar sign. He is someone I owe a great deal to for my life.

If you feel like money is standing in your way of saving your life, I need you to hear me.

Your life is worth more than the debt. You are worth more than money. Your value is that you cannot be replaced in the lives of those who love you, and as morbid as it is, you will spend the money on a funeral if you don't spend it on your healing.

There is beauty even in the ugly. That is an underlying theme in my life, and so it is with the hospital stay. God had been silent in my mind for many months leading up to the stay. I was screaming at him, yelling, swearing, **where are you in all of this**? Where the fuck are you? Why have you abandoned me?

And I found Him again in that cold hospital room. **The neverending tears seemed to unlock the heavens,** even if it were only for one week.

I carried my Bible nearly everywhere in the hospital. I opened it up my first day there in the gym and began trying to focus my eyes through the throbbing pain of a migraine to read the words. I spent nearly the whole time there memorizing Psalms 103:1–5 (NIV). The verses are as follows:

> *¹ Praise the LORD, my soul;*
> *all my inmost being, praise his holy name.*
> *² Praise the LORD, my soul,*
> *and forget not all his benefits—*
> *³ who forgives all your sins*
> *and heals all your diseases,*
> *⁴ who redeems your life from the pit*
> *and crowns you with love and compassion,*
> *⁵ who satisfies your desires with good things*
> *so that your youth is renewed like the eagle's.*

By the time I left the hospital, I had those verses ingrained in my mind. I repeated them over and over. *Praise the Lord, my soul;* **all** *my inmost being, praise his holy name . . . who redeems your life from the pit and crowns you with love and compassion.*

These words I prayed over hourly, minute by minute. Most of the time I had no words, just the plea to be healed.

What is so interesting to me is that people seem to think you are magically healed after you go to the mental hospital, like, *five days just fixed the last eighteen months*. Oh boy, are they wrong! I think I may have even believed I would be more fixed up than I was when I was released. But, it is like putting Band-Aids on the cracks of a fish tank and thinking the Band-Aids will keep all the water from slowly dripping out of the tank and flooding the floor, ultimately leaving your pet fish lifeless.

Fish need the water to live.

Here I was, like this fish in the tank that was all bandaged up but still dripping, and soon I would be all dry, and not in a good way. In a way that seemed to leave no life in me. I was like a zombie going from one task to another, so drugged . . . I wasn't alive and I wasn't dead, either. How was this any better than the pain I was in before?

For months I fought like hell to get out of this indifferent state of mind. I was so numb. I wasn't actually suicidal, but I wouldn't mind if I just died in a car accident, either. I spent months trying to find healing, doing all the things I should do—going to therapy weekly, taking my medication—and still I just fought for the will to live every damn day. I thought walking into the mental hospital meant I was choosing life, but really I was still just choosing not to die.

CHAPTER 10

Groundhog Day

I just want to quit.

I just want to quit.

I hear these words as if they are echoing back to me, like I'm standing on the edge of a cliff and yelling them: *I just want to quit!* But the echo challenges me. It responds by saying, **so do it.**

Oh, the challenge.

Yet, I have a choice! And so do you.

You have the choice to say, "Okay, you gave me permission," *or* you can accept the challenge of living **even not knowing where you are going.**

I remember when each day felt like *Groundhog Day*, repeating the simple activities of just breathing.

I know what it is like to be stuck in a loop. I was there when I was stuck in suicide ideation, feeling haunted by the devil in the thick of psychosis. I would cling to my husband every morning as he tried to leave for work. I would cry and beg him not to go, but he didn't understand how dark a place I was in because I hadn't yet let him in. I would cry because I didn't know if I would see him again. *Would this be our last kiss, our final moment? Would he come home to find me in the closet?* Our children were oblivious to the thought I had put into this. Instead, I would focus on what they needed.

Get them

>snacks,

>drinks,

>put on their favorite show in the basement,

>nurse the baby and snap him into the swing.

And then time this so my husband, not the children, would find me.

I'd be a good mom to make it so they were only parentless for a few minutes before Dad would get home to safely scoop them up in his protective arms.

I was stuck in the loop of fighting to not die. I knew where my husband's gun was and it called to me, **taunting me**: *You could just end it, Brooke. All the pain would end.*

LIES.

The pain wouldn't end. I'd just pass the buck to my husband and kids. The pain will not end until it is processed. Either I could deal with it, or I could add it to the generational trauma for my offspring to have to break.

Several months after my mental hospital stay, I experienced extreme physical pain and paralysis (more on that later). During that time, I became intimately familiar with the loop of pain that keeps you stuck in bed. I know what it is like to wonder, *what's the point of waking up everyday if I can't even get myself to the bathroom? What is my value as a mother if I can't drive my kids to school, hold them when they cry, or even pour syrup on their pancakes?* These simple acts of responsibility that tell my children, **I've got you, I'm here for you.**

At a very basic level, all I could do was be a lump on the couch. I was just a body that moved from one piece of furniture to another to be the adult in the room while the kids had to fend for themselves.

One day I had a terrible migraine and they wanted to ride their bikes so badly. My oldest was only six. I had to be out front with them—you cannot let a six-year-old watch a two-year-old. So, all I did was scoot down the stairs, lifting one leg and putting it on the next step down, scooting on my bum. Thump, thump, thump. Around the corner and down the next seven steps. Thump, thump, thump . . .

Out to the grass. I lay there. I just lay flat on my back wearing a hat and sunglasses because they needed their mother's presence. When they fell and skinned their knees, I couldn't jump up to help them. They had to make their way, crying and limping, to me to lie beside me on the grass. What is the purpose of living a life flat on your back? How did my life have value if this was all it was?

I'd hear it again, the taunts from the gun. I just wanted to give up. This time from a place of desperation, of not being able to live in a body so broken, full of so much pain. How can the human experience be filled with so much of this? Why is my lifetime filled with a hundred lifetimes of stories, and I'm just cresting my thirties?

Your loop might not be chronic pain, or suicide ideation, but it might be. Whatever your *Groundhog Day* is, you can break it. We have so much more choice than we think and I know if you are in psychosis or deep depression, you will argue with me. I would have too. You will say, "Brooke, maybe you have a choice, but I don't." I would have said that too. In fact, I would have bitch-slapped you for having the audacity to say I had a choice in the psychosis because I didn't. Not experiencing it. Not the intrusive thoughts. **I didn't choose those**. I *did* have a choice in healing, though, in asking for help, finding a therapist, breaking the silence that held my shame. **Speaking out**. There I found the power to break the groundhog loop, to break the echo, *I just want to give up,* and I found a new narrative. One of strength, purpose, and healing. I have a choice. I have power within me.

CHAPTER 11

Journaling

Journaling was my lifeline throughout my postpartum psychosis. I journaled a lot growing up. It gave me a relationship with a notebook. I could see how I had used words to help me through the dark times before. When I felt like I couldn't *say* what I really wanted to say, I'd turn to writing poetry. I have lots of poetry notebooks that are like journals to me.

Naturally, I felt like I couldn't tell anyone for such a long time when I was struggling through the psychosis, so I once again turned to my journal. I want to introduce you to the idea that a journal holds no judgment. That is a favorite line of mine. Among those blank pages I began to learn how to be authentic, break trauma loops, let go of beliefs, learn to hear my own thoughts, and learn to hear God again.

I feel called to share some of my journal entries with you here. Please be respectful—respectful of *your* place in healing and knowing—of whether or not you should skip any of these entries. Let these words resonate, assuring you that you are not alone in your darkness, in your despair. Let them be a voice to your pain, let them release emotions. Let them be the words encouraging you to share with someone close to you how you are feeling.

Be brave. If you have not sought help, use these words to support you in finally getting the help you need. I have added resources at the end of this chapter to guide you to what you can do to find the support and healing that is available to you.

Each journal entry I share below feels divinely called to be placed here for you. I filled this journal that I titled, "The Survival," in only four months, writing nearly daily. Sometimes, it felt like the only oxygen in my day. Sometimes, I wrote because I felt like such a broken record.

REMINDER . . . if these entries trigger you, I invite you to take a minute to journal YOUR feelings and thoughts. Take time to take some deep breaths and allow yourself the space and speed that feels good to you.

I was hospitalized on January 25, 2019. The timelines in parentheses for the following journal entries reflect the passage of time from the date I entered the hospital.

Journal Entry: February 2019

(one week after being released from the hospital)

The correlation between my rape and hospital stays . . . the helplessness, hopeless, vulnerable, violated feelings. Both occurred in January.

The hospital saved my life but caused so much damage. I wish they knew. I feel like after I was raped, he had so much control over me. I feel like the hospital holds control over me because of the PTSD. I hope I can find healing. That EMDR helps me move forward. Release the weight I carry. Heal me. Then allow me to move forward and have a better intimate life with Trevor.

I feel like I'm making progress elsewhere. I hope I can turn a corner as spring hits. The new growth and buds sprout. I feel like that is symbolic to what I'm going through.

Journal Entry: April 1, 2019

(two months after being released)

God, I'm really leaning in hard. I want to believe you are enough. I know you have been faithful, but this feels too much. I feel like this is too hard. How will I ever heal from this? Please, Lord, heal me. I know you are my healer.

I'm doing all I can to focus on you and not my pit. I'm praising you through this storm. Please, please heal me. If not, please use all of my mess for your glory. Direct my every step. Make me brave in you, Lord, to create change. To help others heal. To be a light to someone else.

Jesus, you've done so much for me. I know you've never failed me. Please pull me from this pit. Redeem me in your holy name. Give me hope. Give me your light. I know you will in your timing. Your timing is never wrong.

Please meet our financial needs. I need Trevor home still. I'm not healed enough to be a mom all the time. Just breathing feels so hard most days. Lord, please provide.

God, my faith feels weak. I've been struggling for so long. Please show me you are here through this storm.

Journal Entry: April 26, 2019

(three months after being hospitalized)

I'm finally seeing improvements, but still, I feel it's a long journey to go. I've had much better days. More stable state. I think the new meds are finally working.

I'm starting to find joy in things again. Gardening, my animals, watching the kids play, sometimes. . . . The other day, I took them on a bike ride and it was fun for me. First time in two years. I used to love doing things like that with the boys.

I've also felt a little sad this week. Probably processing stuff from last therapy. But also feeling extra clingy to Trevor. Needing reassurance we are good and he's not going anywhere. I know he's not. I know we have a good marriage, but it's been hard since he left me at the hospital. I have separation anxiety.

Journal Entry: May 2, 2019

I feel like I can't face this. The hospital stay was the most awful experience of my life because it was trauma on top of trauma. They wouldn't listen to what I was saying and turned everything into a negative.

I can't look at pictures from this winter. I can't see pregnancy or baby stuff. It just hurts. It makes me feel sorry for anyone going through that.

Yesterday and today I've felt like I'd rather die than face the hospital stuff and that it would've been better for me to die than to have gone through that. I know it's not true. I don't want to take a second from Trevor and me, but I don't know how to deal with this. How to face this?

I have a two-week break from therapy now and it scares me. A lot can go on in two weeks.

My thoughts scare me. They can spiral so fast. I've worked so damn hard to climb out of this pit and I feel like drowning doesn't describe how I feel.

Lord, pull me through this.

Journal Entry: May 10, 2019

(A poem about watching other mothers love motherhood and the truth I feel about postpartum mental health)

I feel jealous when I see you
bonding and smiling at your kids.
I can tell now when it's sincere.

I feel jealous when moms
Haven't struggled with the
Darkness I have
but happy
For them too.
I wouldn't wish this on anyone.

I feel annoyed
When someone claims on social media
A little regular exercise cured their postpartum depression
Because mine's much worse than that
And exercise doesn't even touch it.

I feel alone because nobody
Can understand the depth of my pain.
The hell I'm trying to survive.
The PTSD that
Haunts me day and nights

I feel grateful for finally
Finding right medical team
to help me and listen to me.
About what medication adjustment I need.

Doctors who answer their phone on a weekend
To let me talk
Because he knows it can't wait.

A therapist who is trained to handle postpartum mood disorders
And reassure me through the setbacks
And has been there for me even through vacations
Because she understands the delicate place I'm in.

I'm grateful for the friends who've shown up unannounced
Just to sit with me,
Or to listen to me vent about my struggles.

Grateful for the friends who've said they are coming over
And just start cleaning,
Folding laundry,
Or doing the dishes.
You help without judgment.

This is my reality.
This is my darkness,
This pain, this jealousy.

I've had to unfollow you
Because your joy for life hurts me more.

I'm on multiple medications just to function
At a basic level and will be for life.
This doesn't make me a bad mom
Or less of one.
It makes me strong for
Recognizing I need that
And makes me a better wife and friend.

I work each day to dig myself out of this hole
With the most amazing husband as my support.
I couldn't have asked for better support from him
He's listened,
He's held me as I cried for hours
Day and night
He's promised me I'll make it through this
And done what he's had to, to ensure I do.
Without him, I wouldn't be here today to write this.

Once I saw someone post
'just remember, postpartum depression doesn't kill.'
I want to tell her how wrong she is.
You can't control the intrusive thoughts that come in your mind
You may want to live in your heart
But the pain in your chest will drive you to insanity.
But I'm a survivor
Despite our broken medical system.
I've survived,
I'm not healed but I'm here.

Unnamed Poem, Final Draft: May 16, 2019

(A poem I wrote in my journal processing my mental hospital stay)

If only these walls
Would tumble down.
Would I find myself
In this place?

These walls haunt me.
These tears a
Constant reminder
You're not here

This pain in my chest
Is no longer
From this darkness
But because I'm
Doing this alone.

The strength within
The will to live,
I'll have to find a way.

Misunderstood, unheard.
How can you be here to help?

You've taken so much from me.
You've caused me pain.
You've controlled me long enough.

I won't let you take me down.
You'll make me stronger.
You'll empower me
You'll cause me to create change

You no longer haunt me
You no longer control me
You no longer define me.

Because of you
I'll make a difference.
Because of you
I've found my passion
Because of you
I've found my place.

Poem: "What You See," May 31, 2019

(A poem about experiencing postpartum psychosis alone—I was shocked to hear people thought I had all my shit together, and I was drowning.)

You see the smile

All I see is the pain

You see the happy pictures

All I see is the mask

That I put on

Those that know

Think I'm recovering

They don't really know

It's only getting worse

The trauma is piling up

And they think

The meds have fixed it all

I still see the pain

Behind every fake smile

I still see the struggle

I'm trying not to show

> *I still see the pain*
> *Piercing through my heart*
>
> *You've stopped reaching out*
> *Because you think it's all done*
> *But for me the healing's just begun.*

I have no idea where reading those left you emotionally. I reread these and I see so much strength. I see so much anger, hurt, and pain, but mostly I see how much overcoming, healing, and possibilities that letting these words out provided me.

If you do not journal, I encourage you to pick up a journal now. In fact, I am giving you space here, right now, in this book, to process any emotions reading those journal entries may have brought up. Let them pour out onto these pages alongside my words, and let it be a safe landing place for them to rest.

LINK TO RESOURCES

A Journal Holds No Judgment

A Journal Holds No Judgment

A Journal Holds No Judgment

CHAPTER 12

You Have More Choice than You Think You Do

Journaling will be the journey you take to clear out the path ahead of you. Up until now, if your trauma has been creating a loop, it is hard to choose anything else. Journaling is step one to clearing the loop. To completely heal the trauma loops, you will need support from a certified therapist, healer, or guide.

This requires that you acknowledge that you are important enough to invest in.

When I share with people that I am working with a publisher that offers amazing author support, I am often surprised by their second response. Initially, they express how wonderful it is, but then they always ask about the price. When I reveal the cost of my package, I am often taken aback by how many people are unwilling to invest that much in themselves.

I also struggle with investing in myself, but for different reasons. Many people say, "Well, if you have that much lying around, then that's great that you can afford to invest in that!"

The reality is, we didn't just "have that much money lying around" for a rainy day, or in this case, for the day I finally decided to pursue my dreams. I had enough for the first installment and a husband crazy enough to love and believe in me, saying "I was just waiting for you to ask."

That's another story.

I firmly believe that if I step up to do what God has called me to do and align myself with it, IF I take the steps of faith and action, THEN God will provide. Much like the law of gravity—I don't have to understand gravity for it to apply to me. The only difference between you and me may be that I have the boxes of failed business attempts sitting in my garage. *Seriously, I do!* We have had many failed business ventures, each teaching us something about ourselves or business and narrowing down our passions each step of the way. We may have failed multiple times, but I don't see them as failures. Each "failure" has brought us deeper faith and strength. I have found that investing in myself is one of the ways I replenish my cup. I invest in support, and that support takes me to the next level of growth I seek.

So many people don't want to take the first step in life without a guarantee, but life just isn't meant to be lived that way. The thing that makes life such an adventure is that there are no guarantees. There are no promises for a happily ever after. There is heartache, pain, sickness. There are children who suffer unthinkable pains, and that can cause you to yell at God and ask where He is in all of this.

For each failed venture we have had so much growth and learning. You see, if I am paying my publisher for a service and wanting dollar-for-dollar that investment matched or returned in profit, I am living in a lack mindset. I am not seeing the value she and her team bring to the table beyond the value of a dollar. If I live life trading my time for the dollar, I will never move past the borders of lack mindset, and I will forever let fear, instead of faith, govern my decisions. I do expect that the education I get writing this book, the friendships I've developed, and the confidence I build will be more than the value a dollar could ever hold. This process is teaching me to step into the best version of myself, the Brooke who is confident enough in herself to step onto a stage, to share the dark, scary, embarrassing parts of my life story. The parts that shame would rather convince me are unlovable; they are the unthinkable monsters in the closet and they will stop people from loving and accepting me. If I let that lie rule my life, I will never step out in confidence with the message I have been called to share! Shame on me if I let fear and shame rule my future!

Sitting in shame is just like sitting in lack. It's mucky, muddy, and messy. I have to invest in people and programs that see me as my best self. My best self six months from now, even. That gives me a place to *practice feeling safe* in my future self. That teaches me *how to feel safe* in my future self.

I know how scary it is to take that first step investing in your healing, your therapy, or your dreams. Your thoughts immediately go to lack, the place of fearing failure, or having guilt for spending money on yourself instead of your kids' dreams. We fall prey to the lies that somehow, because we are adults and have adult responsibilities, our dreams no longer hold importance.

That is a lie.

I am here to remind you that you are worth investing in. IF that first step is healing, getting help, or investing in your dreams—you are worthy of it! Do not look at your investment penny-for-penny: do not expect to get a penny back for every penny spent, because that is limiting thinking. What you gain may be growth as a person rather than growth in finances, growing into the person who then can share the message, share their story, to help others heal. Investing in writing this book was not the first step I took to writing this book. Choosing to heal was, and that was a choice that took conscious effort.

You have so many more choices available to you than you realize. You just have to practice making the choices and allowing each one to open up more. The life you currently live is not your only choice. YOU have the agency and ability to choose something different from your current circumstances.

CHAPTER 13

Choosing to Live

The gift of sharing our stories is that we don't have to go through the hard thing to allow it to change our lives. Today, I am going to unpack a story with you. I really haven't spent much time unraveling this experience. I have actually only uttered the words a few times in my life. What words, you ask? *I had a near-death experience.* I have downplayed this event because it was so different from the ones you might think of initially. I don't know what heaven is like. I never saw God's face, or even the angel for that matter. **I just know I died and I had to choose to come back.**

I started writing my book weeks before this near-death experience, which occurred on April 8, 2020. It was the day I was supposed to be having my fusion but because of Covid, my fusion surgery had been postponed.

This day started just like any other. I woke up in extreme pain. As I woke up, I remembered that it was not all a dream. The only reason I could even sleep was thanks to medication. I couldn't do anything for my throbbing pain. It felt like a nuclear bomb had gone off in my head and the aftershocks traveled down my neck that was held tightly in an Aspen Vista tx neck brace, which I was in 24-7. Sleeping, showers, changing, eating . . . it didn't matter. If I planned to keep breathing, I was in it. If I were to take it off, my head would collapse, and within two minutes I would have no control over my body, no eyesight even. I wouldn't be able to talk. Though I couldn't ever feel my body, the neckbrace held my head in a false sense of security, allowing me to continue to have some control over my limbs.

On this day, the sun was shining so brightly it hurt my eyes and skin as I used my crutches to make my way slowly to the car. I lived in sunglasses and hats to help, but it was never enough. Even in a pitch-black room, my eyes would scream in pain. My husband was driving me to physical therapy. Usually my mom drove me, but since Covid had shut everything down almost a month before, she hadn't been the one driving me. So on this day, Trevor was driving me. It was unusual that he was the one driving me. I cherished the extra time in his company. He did so much to take care of me and the boys, providing and filling in for me when I couldn't. Whenever I was in this much pain, it was nice to just have him there. His company is calming.

We got to PT and walked in. The staff could tell I was in a lot of pain. They could see it on my face, even though I gave them a big smile. They asked how I was and I shot back, "Better, now I'm here. Hoping

Matt can work his magic today!" They told me a room was open and I could head back.

I wobbled my way to the room. I had the rhythm of a three-legged dog. I walked with one forearm crutch most of the time. On bad days, you may have seen me with two, but it felt nice to be confident in my ability to walk using only one on that day. A tech brought in the heating pads and asked me how my pain was. I responded with, "Zero stars, would not recommend." When asked this question multiple times a week, I decided I needed to get creative in my responses. Saying ten-, fourteen-, or even fifteen-out-of-ten was just not cutting it anymore.

Ten minutes. That's how long the timer was set for the heat. Matt would come in after the timer sounded and he would work on me. The door was left cracked because I needed the lights off, even while wearing my sunglasses. I mourned not being able to remove my neck brace for heat anymore. I used to be able to manage to take it off when lying down, but it had been months since I'd been able to do that. I just tried to tuck some of my back heat up under my brace a little.

I don't remember how long into the timer it had been or what I had even been thinking about when I realized I had gone into paralysis again. I tried to speak but couldn't. I'd never lost my ability to talk while wearing my neck brace before. I could blink, but that wasn't helpful in a dark room while I was wearing sunglasses. I couldn't move my arms or legs to get Trevor's attention. I thought, *oh well, they will figure it out when Matt walks in.* It was then that I began to feel much like a balloon. With each breath, I felt like my body was filling up with air— just packing it in, starting at my toes and filling up my legs in the next breath. The overwhelming amount of peace and calm I felt in that moment was my first clue: I was dying. That was it. I was startled by having no urgency to fight back. I was surrendering. Each breath got a bit more shallow than the previous one. Then my hands and arms were being filled. I was so full of oxygen that I felt like what the Pillsbury Doughboy must feel like. Amid my extreme peace, I felt a tinge of sadness. Trevor was right there and I just wanted to tell him how grateful I am for his love, his patience, his attention, his fight for me. He'd sacrificed so much to save my life the last few years and here we were. I just wanted him to know I saw it all. I saw it. I saw him . . . *I see you babe. Thank you.*

Then somewhere in my last tiny gasp of air my logical brain kicked in and said, "Why are you dying now? You just fought like hell to survive postpartum psychosis. You wrestled the devil for eighteen months, then spent seven more months just fighting to live everyday after that till things finally got easier. Just a year ago, you were still fighting to choose to live everyday, and now you are going to just give up? You did not survive that to just die on this table, Brooke!"

By then I was looking down on my body and my husband. He was looking down at his phone and my spirit was pleading that he knew my heart, that he knew how much I loved him, how much I appreciated him, and how grateful I was that he drove me that day so I could spend my last moments with him. Then it went black. All black. There was nothing. Silence, not even a thought.

"It's not your time yet, Brooke."

Someone else's voice had just appeared in my mind. There was nobody around. No family greeting me at the gates. Just a faceless angel talking to my mind directly . . . using theirs? I don't know. "What? How is it not my time? I'm dead."

"Brooke, I can't make you go back, but you need to. You need to go back. It's not your time. Breathe."

"I don't want to go back to that body! I am already here and I'm at peace with it. Just let me be. I can't breathe. There is no room left in that body for air. It is full." I was not exactly talking, more just thinking out loud, or maybe not out loud and just to the angel.

I don't know that they said much more. I just remember hearing them say, "You have to try to breathe. You have to try!" I could hear the urgency in their tone, the plea they were trying to give me. I remember reluctantly saying that I would try one time. That's all.

Just like that I was snapped back to my body. It still felt full, but I tried again to breathe in. It didn't feel like I got much air, but just the tad I got created a hunger in my veins for more, and it was urgent. I began to try to breathe more. Each breath got a little deeper, a little stronger.

Then, my consciousness returned and I became aware that Matt was in the room trying to talk to me. Trevor was standing up because of my lack of response . . . then the seizure started.

I had been struggling with instability seizures for the previous nine months (at least), but since being in the neck brace around the clock, I'd rarely had them. This one felt like a shockwave pulsing through my body, the fight I was in to reclaim my life. It lasted forty minutes in all. Matt worked with me to calm my nervous system. He later told me how terrifying this day was, but you would not have known he was terrified at the time. He seemed collected to me, granted I wasn't all there.

As I began to regain control of my body, my arm movement returned before my speech did. I tried signing to Trevor that I had died but he didn't understand. Sign language wasn't his thing. Once I was able to move my fingers a bit more, I reached for my phone and started typing out in my notes that I had died and he said, "No, you didn't. I was here the whole time. We checked your heart too, babe." Which they had . . . after I came back.

We really have no understanding still as to what triggered that episode medically. Spiritually, though, I sit with it. I wrestle with it.

You see, it is a full spectrum. For the two years prior to this experience, I'd had to choose to not die, almost daily. I would say that January 25, 2019, at 11 p.m. is when I chose to live because that is when I walked myself into a mental hospital hand-in-hand with my husband, knowing

I could not allow him to spend the rest of his life questioning if he could have done more to save my life had I ultimately committed suicide that night. It was terrible. I couldn't even take a drink without him checking my mouth for pills that day. Couldn't walk to the bathroom alone because I saw a chemical cleaner, high out of reach of the littles, just within my reach. . . . I just wanted my emotional pain to end. So, I willingly walked into a mental hospital because I could not put the weight of "what if I had . . ." in his mind. I could not allow him to feel responsible for not being able to save me.

So, on a cold dark winter night in January, I *thought* I had chosen to live. The reality is, I had *chosen not to die*. It was on that bright sunny day in April—a day that was just as painful as that dark night in January—that I actually *chose to live*, not just to not die. I chose to come back to this crippled body. The angel had made one thing clear: I hadn't fulfilled my purpose yet, but they could not *make* me return to my broken home. I had a choice. I chose life! Even in that pain, even in the heartache, the uncertainty that was my future. That is why I am writing this book: to fully live, not *just* breathe.

What does it mean to choose to live?

I had a choice to make. I wasn't forced to return to my body. I chose to. What is most interesting to me is I chose to return to a body that was so broken. It felt beyond repair. I chose to live even knowing this was my future. Even not knowing when I would have surgery. I wondered, *why did I have this experience and what does it mean to choose to live?* This is the message that has to be shared.

I hear about other people's near-death experiences and I wonder why mine was the way it was. No bright light, no visible angels, just complete peace, no fear.

When I made the choice to come back to my body, I thought of my boys. My children were so young. My baby was only two. I thought about how much I had left to teach them, love on them, and how many kisses and hugs they still needed from me, but most importantly I needed to teach them how to live even with. . . . Even with a neck brace. Even with being in paralysis. Even with the physical pain and mental anguish I had faced. NOT even *if* . . . but even WITH. *With* because this was my now, and now is all we have.

How can I teach them the beauty, the magic, and the holiness of actually living even WITH? That is the miracle, that I chose to learn to live *even with* and find purpose, joy, and even healing from that place.

So how do we choose to live even with?

First, it *is* a choice. A conscious choice.

Second, making this choice won't fix anything overnight, but it will open your heart. It will allow your heart to align with God, to align with your higher purpose in this life. You begin to BE and not *do*. We are human BEINGS. Our power comes from being who we are, even if we don't accomplish anything on the to-do list each day. **It is our presence in other people's lives that makes us so special.**

When beginning to live intentionally, you will have mental pushback. This is new to your brain and nervous system. Because of this, you may feel unsafe. Living intentionally might feel exhausting, but don't give up. Soon it will feel more freeing, more in alignment with who you are meant to be, and you will find within you a joy and peace that is like an unfamiliar heaven. I believe this is how life was meant to be lived.

CHAPTER 14

Let's Talk Miracles

I struggle with the phrase *tender mercy*. Growing up as a member of the LDS religion, I heard it often, but it never sat right with me. It felt as though we weren't giving God enough credit. Like, let's call them what they are: MIRACLES! That feels right.

What are miracles?

A miracle is as simple as waking up in the morning with breath in your lungs. It is phoning a friend when you feel like you should. It is turning right while driving in the car when your brain says to turn left, only to find out later there was a car accident that collided around the time you would have been turning left. *That could have been you.*

A miracle is being in the right place at the right time. My husband seems to roll up on car accidents often. He has the training to handle those situations and to manage the scene until cops arrive. He is a miracle in the life of the person who was in the car accident.

Miracles, some big, some small, are contagious and carry the most beautiful frequency in them. I know we tend to downplay them by calling them things like "tender mercies" and comparing the size of the miracle to the size of your neighbor's miracle. You've probably heard the saying a time or two, but it's worth repeating: *comparison is the thief of joy.*

Is it a miracle I am standing and walking today? ABSOLUTELY! Does this discredit or minimize any miracle in your life? NO! Big fat HELL NO!

I challenge you to start practicing calling miracles out throughout your day. Train yourself to see them. Each sunrise and sunset you get to witness, see it as a miracle. Let God show off the beauty in His creations.

Each time you hear a child laugh, *let the miracle of that life created echo through your mind.*

Each injury that should have been worse, pause and speak that miracle into this realm. I know there is so much power in sharing miracles. Miracles were not just happening when Jesus physically walked this earth. Miracles should be an everyday occurrence in our lives.

The problem with humans is we forget. OH, we forget so easily. Why do you think we see patterns in the Bible? We forget what precious miracles we see each day and we begin to take them for granted. We don't see them for all the beauty they actually are.

One way we can combat this is to speak miracles into existence with gratitude. Get in the habit of marking them, like a vocal marker in the moment the miracle is happening. Catching the flowers blooming, stretching open in the morning sunlight—that's a miracle!

I write of this because often when you have battled chronic illness or mental health disorders for a long time, you lose the ability to see the good in the world around you. Everything is out to get you rather than everything is working for you. We have to train our minds and our eyes to see the good and beauty again. We need to teach our minds how to create new ways of thinking and of seeing the world.

At first, this will feel like a dangerous endeavor to your nervous system. Don't let it fool you; this is the greatest gift you can give yourself. You will soon find that, like a muscle, it is easy to flex and engage it when you need to change your energy. To truly embrace healing, you need to adjust your frequency to a higher vibration.

Let miracles cleanse and calm you like rain calms forest fires. Like a mother's touch soothes a baby. Miracles are the calm to the nervous system. Soak this in. Let miracles put out the doubt.

> The doubt that God is there.
>
> The doubt that He cares for you.
>
> The doubt that you are worthy of His love, mercy, grace, and love.

Let miracles teach you of His nature. Rest. Rest in His nature. Do not be distracted by your surroundings calling to you. Do not let the world shut God out. This is a call to open the heavens and let God share His divine power with us. We need only ask.

There are so many miracles that I have experienced that I could share. Some are so simple, like asking my son if there was anything he wanted to talk about when it was past our usual bedtime and he completely opened up to me—something that a pre-teen doesn't do easily. For a moment, I felt blessed as a mother that I had put down my exhaustion and asked, and my child had opened up his heart and answered. In those moments, I know God is working with me as a mother.

Other miracles really are crazy miraculous, like the fact that I even have four children. I went through seven pregnancies to bring these four boys to earth. When I was seventeen, a doctor recommended that I have a hysterectomy. That doctor felt my chances of conceiving were so low and my medical complications from my monthly cycle were severe enough to suggest this surgery to a child. I gave birth to my first miracle less than two years later.

This leads me to my next miracle. At eighteen, when I started having kids, I had no firm answers for the varying health problems I had been experiencing since age twelve. One of the diagnoses I had yet to receive could have led me to becoming paralyzed during any normal delivery. The pressure on my spinal cord when the baby was passing through the birth canal could have left me paralyzed for life. Yet, after each baby I was walking within minutes of birthing. I would begin running again as soon as I was cleared.

These babies, the process of bringing them to earth, is a miracle within itself, but when I had these unknown conditions that could have complicated the situation, I thank God that much more for the miracles that are mine.

Seven years after my first baby was born I found myself unwell and trending downward quickly. One weekend I was running eight to ten miles because I loved it so much, and the next weekend I was lying in a hospital bed unable to even speak. All I could do was blink. *All I could do was blink.*

It was the fall of 2019 and three or four months prior I had begun to be very dizzy and pass out regularly. Something as simple as getting too hot in the garden made me pass out. There were many days I did not feel safe to drive and would ask Trevor to take the kids to school. In the middle of August that year I woke up with a migraine one day, and it just never left. For two weeks I would have headaches varying from severe to migraine, then have one day pain free, just for the pain to return the next day.

I was in early communication with my family doctor about the many neurological symptoms that were appearing: spotty vision, blurred vision, tingling in my limbs. Then, one evening while I was at the hospital for imaging, I lost feeling in my legs. The images came back normal, and I cried the first of many tears I would shed in fear and frustration.

By Friday night (a few days after getting the imaging), my speech had gotten sketchy. I couldn't always speak when I wanted to and when I did, it was very slow and robotic. It felt like it took me a whole minute just to spit out one sentence. Even more frustrating was that I would forget what word I was trying to say midword. Trevor would finish the word for me and most of the time I couldn't remember I was even trying to say anything. Or I just felt like I was in the middle of doing something and forgot. That something was talking to him. It took so much energy to just exist again—to try and do anything, from thinking to speaking.

That Friday night I visited my doctor to go over what was happening, and he suggested we go to the ER and get more imaging done. He was not satisfied with the imaging that had been completed a few days before because something was drastically wrong. I stood up and couldn't move. I took deep breaths, tried to be calm, focused, and could see my feet moving in my mind, but my feet would not actually move. I sat down again and tried to move my legs. Still, they would not move. No matter how hard I thought about it, they couldn't do it. This is the first time I was picked up and moved into a wheelchair. My husband took me to the hospital. I was back to not being able to speak or move at all. Even my arms could not listen to my brain. What was going on?

I spent a day in the hospital. I was admitted and CAT scans were performed and a spinal tap collected. Many dangerous viruses were ruled out that weekend, but still no answer was found. I had my hunch of what was going on. My family has a history of Chiari malformation. This is when the brain is slipping out of the skull and into the spinal cord opening. This puts pressure on the brain, blocks off communication, and can cause a backup of spinal fluid that causes pressure to build in the brain.

The neurologist on call literally looked me in the eyes and said, "It does not matter if you have family history of this," (my sister to be exact), "that is not your problem. Your problem is your postpartum depression is returning and we would like to hospitalize you."

Trevor and I made eye contact and laughed. *Laughed*. We both knew I was very stable and I had just had an appointment with my psychiatrist two weeks prior that had gone so well we didn't need to make medication adjustments. I was still in weekly therapy and my therapist was so pleased with my healing. I knew in my heart this doctor was way off base and that I needed to follow my instincts from there.

All of this was leading up to some of the biggest miracles to happen in my life to date. I can speak of miracles because each day, I am one. I am a ***walking*** miracle. This was just the beginning to the most amazing string of miracles to happen yet on my path to Barcelona.

CHAPTER 15

The Path to Barcelona

I married a saint. I am convinced of it. I understand how rare it really is to break the abuse cycles. Statistically, I should have ended up in an abusive relationship. I know God protected me because I needed a man like Trevor so I could do this work that I was called to do.

Trevor doesn't flinch. He is someone who rolls with the punches. His dad once described Trevor's childhood self as someone who, if he found out their house was burning down and was going to be lost, he would bring the marshmallows to make one more good memory from it.

This is one of the things I so deeply love about him.

I was not naturally this way. I was thick skinned, tough, and braced for each punch. Trevor taught me safety and how to let things roll off my back. Through his safe presence, I began to shed the tough skin and find strength in my feminine power.

I share this because by the time we experienced my paralysis, we were seasoned like a well-oiled cast-iron pan. We had four kids together, had done moves and remodels together, and survived postpartum psychosis together. None of it tore us apart; it all brought us closer because we were determined to not be broken through it.

The doctor at the hospital believed it was my postpartum depression recurring just six weeks after I was truly being me again, and just nine months since I had been hospitalized. He wanted to put me back in inpatient care until I could learn to walk again and learn to handle life. Trevor and I laughed out loud. We looked at each other and said to the doctor, "We could have handed you your diagnosis. We knew once you saw that, you would not look for the real cause of this." Trevor firmly, safely, and confidently said to him, "You will discharge her or I will sign an AMA." That means to leave against medical advice. I have never been discharged so quickly from the hospital. I got a copy of our imaging and testing from the weekend there and we drove home.

Once we were home, Trevor pulled up on the grass and lovingly placed me on our steps. He told me not to move because he was going to park the truck on the side of the house. So, stubborn Brooke, who had recently regained control of but not feeling in her arms, started sliding her way up the stairs to the front door. This was my reality now, and I was determined to figure out how to live like this.

He was not surprised at all to find me sitting in front of the door. He knew my stubborn heart all too well after eight years of marriage. So, he opened the door and I scooted just inside to lean, panting, against the wall. My boys yelled, "Mom!" and embraced me. And so it began, this journey of being told I was crazy but knowing this time in my being that I was, in fact, *not* crazy. I had to fight for the real medical help I needed. I had a knowing in my body though—the knowing that I was not crazy this time. There was a real problem and I had to get to the bottom of it. Once I fell into paralysis, it would take months of fighting to receive proper medical treatment.

My first morning home after being in the hospital I woke to the pressure of a full bladder. My eyes burned in pain; I could feel my heartbeat with each throb of my headache. Trevor was still peacefully sleeping and I did not want to wake him to help me. He had just helped me through so much as I had fought postpartum psychosis. I felt like the least I could do for him was let him sleep in. So, pleasantly surprised to find I could still move my arms, I rolled out of bed and did a funny crawl that resembled an army crawl but without moving my legs. Out of breath, I made it to the toilet, just to realize I had to now pick myself up off the floor to get on the toilet. I firmly placed my hands on either side of the toilet seat and began to just pull my body up, shifting weight to one hand as I moved the other to twist my body and place myself squarely on the seat. I now saw how helpful a bar could be if this became a long-term issue. When I finished relieving myself on the toilet, I kind of just pushed myself off the toilet and caught myself on my hands and knees. Then I began to scoot to the bathroom counter, held onto the sink, and pulled myself up to a locked hip position. I slowly let go of bracing myself with the sink and found my knees could support me. So I got ready that morning on my knees.

Then I quietly scooted across my room and to the top of the stairs. I lifted each leg one at a time, putting each leg one or two steps down in front of me, then scooting my butt down to the next step, repeating this all the way down the stairs. I paused at the bottom of the stairs before scooting across the family room to pull myself up on the couch. I lay there with a hot pad for my pain and wearing a soft-collar neck brace to try and support my heavy head. I couldn't move because of the pure pain and exhaustion from getting myself to the couch.

The previous evening I had overnighted a hard-collar neck brace to myself. While I was still in the hospital the day before, I had begun researching and believed I had a genetic disorder called Ehlers-Danlos Syndrome (EDS), and that combined with the head injury I sustained at age six (that left me color-blind), the neck injury at I had at age fifteen (that had me in a soft-collar brace for five weeks), *and* my seven pregnancies had led to the instability I was now having in my neck. Additionally, I suspected a Chiari malformation. Getting this hard-collar neck brace was the first step to regaining my life.

Once I was in the hard-collar neck brace for a few hours my pain level dropped a couple points, leaving me functioning at around a 7–8 on a 10-point scale pain chart. This felt like such a relief and gave me hope that I could possibly survive until I could manage to have the surgery I suspected I needed. After being in the hard-collar brace for a day and lying on a disc hydrator device, I began to regain movement in my feet—just a couple inches off the ground at first.

When Monday rolled around (just two days after my ER visit), I texted my mother and asked her to hunt down some forearm crutches for me. I knew if I could lift my feet three inches off the floor, even without feeling, that meant I could learn to walk again. Trevor confirmed with my mom that if she didn't do it, I would track down someone else to find me some, so she might as well. Stubborn Brooke was not going to back down without a fight.

By Monday afternoon, just three days after paralysis had set in, I found myself trying to figure out how to get off the gray couch that my kids once played on while I worked out. This time, though, I couldn't even stand by myself. I had to have Trevor help me up and balance on my "new" legs. We set the crutches to the right height and I began to scoot my feet along the carpet, moving one crutch at a time. Then one leg at a time. I could not believe it. I was moving my legs! This was the first of many miracles to follow.

I spent days watching medical lectures—those lectures specialty doctors put on to do continuing education with other doctors. I took pages of notes. Ultimately, I am blessed with an amazing family doctor who'd fought to save my life just nine months before. I would call him up and say, "I need to get this image done and they don't have any in the state of Utah." So, he would write the order for me to go to Las Vegas or Colorado to get the imaging I needed. I found a list of specialists that could perform my surgery, and only two were in America. Both of them declined my case. One of them did not give me a reason, and the other I said it was because I did not have the right insurance. There again, my life was being dictated by the little rectangular card in my wallet. My worth to them just came down to this card.

So I pushed on. The next option was a doctor in Barcelona, Spain. It seemed so crazy, traveling halfway around the world for surgery, but he was my next hope. I submitted all my paperwork and waited to hear from him. Meanwhile, I continued to decline. The week of Thanksgiving in 2019, I got all my documents and imaging submitted to him. My husband applied for his passport (I already had mine), and we waited. Weeks of waiting, not knowing how long it would take, and me still in constant pain. The week of Christmas I took a drastic turn for the worse. I felt a nudge. I felt I should email this doctor's assistant and tell her how much worse I was getting, that now instability seizures had started and they were intense. I wasn't sure what would come from it, but I had faith.

So Christmas passed. I watched my kids open their presents like I was an outsider in their lives. Like they lived their life and I lived inside a Mason jar. I had a clear view of them but was unable to actually touch them and interact with them. My autoimmune disorder caused me to feel so stuck in my body, like a prisoner in a dungeon with no light to the outside. That Christmas was painful for me. I struggled with the feeling that I was just watching my kids grow up without their mother. *Why did I survive psychosis for this? Why did I survive psychosis if I was going to let this take me down?* So, the fire lived on in me, fighting for life.

On New Year's Eve, I received an email from the doctor in Barcelona. He had a diagnosis for me, confirming what my gut had told me all along: I wasn't crazy. In fact, my head was barely hanging on to my spine. My cervical spine compression was severe, and he wanted to schedule a skype call with me. I couldn't believe it. God saw me! This doctor wanted to give me a fighting chance.

Two weeks later, I set my alarm for 3 a.m. I was to meet with him in the middle of the night because of the time difference between our countries.

He jumped on the call, and I remember thinking this must be a dream. After reviewing my imaging I sent to him, as well as the answers I had given to his questionnaire, he had the most shocking news for me. Surely, this doctor didn't just say I was a "textbook case of EDS, cervical instability, and Mast Cell Activation Syndrome (MCAS)"! Holy shit! I had never been told I was a textbook case before. My husband looked as shocked and disbelieving as I felt.

We wrapped up the call and got a tiny bit more sleep before our young kids woke us. It was sometime in the following days that the surgery proposal landed in my email. It was going to be about $80,000 with the current exchange rate. Without hesitation Trevor said, "If this feels right to you, then ask them what we need to do to get on the schedule." So I did. They gave me the details: how much to pay up front to get on the schedule and when it would need to be paid in full. I couldn't believe it. We would need to pay in full before even flying out there for me to have surgery. I didn't know how we were going to pay for it. There was no way we could. Then Trevor, as cool as a cucumber, with his sparkling eyes looked deep into mine and said matter-of-factly, "We will just sell the house."

What?! Just like that? No biggy?

And so we did.

The pathway of miracles began to unfold, one of them being that the assistant that worked for this surgeon was from Provo, UT. My hometown, the town I was currently living in. She had spent twenty years in Provo, had met her husband in Provo, and was now working and living in Barcelona, Spain. I was the first American patient they had, and I was from her hometown. This was a miracle to me. Someone who understood my language, my culture, and had even walked the streets I called home was going to be with me through this process every step of the way. God prepared this years before I collapsed. While I was still fighting psychosis, He was preparing her family to move to Spain and be there for me.

CHAPTER 16

Selling the House

The house had been on the market for weeks. We were running out of time to sell it. We had open houses, showings, and we were down to just shy of a month before we needed to pay for my surgery in full. I just leaned into faith and let there be no room for doubt. Just like the miracle it was, someone made an offer on our house. From listing to closing was about two months, but most offers, once accepted, take three weeks to close. This did not give us much wiggle room for a possible contract cancellation and still be able to meet the deadline for paying for my surgery.

The buyers scheduled to close two days before we needed to wire the money to Barcelona. The closing happened smoothly, without any hiccups. We wired the money the day after it hit our bank account, and we moved into a one-bedroom basement apartment with our four boys the day Utah shut down for two weeks for Covid-19.

It was Friday, March 17, 2020.

SELLING THE HOUSE

My kids didn't have school that Friday and they were helping us move. My oldest was seven years old and in first grade. My baby was two. We set up two bunk beds in the family room and my husband and I were in the one bedroom, and the computer was in our bedroom, so our room doubled as his office. We did much of our children's crisis schooling from the bedroom, bringing their work up onto my bed. This felt like such an impossible feat. Yet, somehow, each day I managed to teach them the bare minimum. Not by my strength, but by God's. Much like He had carried me through many dark days, He was carrying me through something else that felt impossible.

Some days, I managed to go out to the kitchen. I would set up the laptops and sit the kids down around the kitchen table that was too big for the tiny apartment. I put the boys at opposite ends of the table, one working on science, the other on math. I would sit next to the preschooler, who was doing packets, and the two year old, who didn't want to feel left out. I often looked rather rough. I used humor to get through these hard days and would joke I was a Hollywood star hiding out behind the sunglasses and hat I had to use to help shield me from the light. I would just rotate between helping each kid as they had questions or needed guidance or encouragement. Every day I did this until my nervous system just couldn't take anymore, then we would stop and call it as good as it was going to get.

Then, I would lie in the backyard while they played. They would play on the swingset and the airplane teeter-totter, the one I used to play on with them. They would go down the slides I used to go down, and swing on the swings I used to push them on. All of those times felt like lifetimes ago. Now, all I could do was hobble out there with my forearm crutches, wearing my neck brace that felt like a sleeping bag around my neck, and sit in the sun while wearing my hat and dark sunglasses. Often I was under an umbrella, too, as I was also experiencing neuropathy. When the sun hit my skin it would feel like fire had erupted. So, I would hide in the shade the best I could. Sometimes I would lie on the cool grass and other times on the oversized cement steps that led down to the basement apartment door. I would lie there on my back with my eyes closed and listen to my boys play—listen to them, and they would ask for me to watch. If I were to look it would require me to move my whole body onto my side to see them. I could not just look to my left like everybody else could. I would gently remind them of this and slowly move myself to my side for a few minutes to watch each of them show me something. I would celebrate them and then slowly roll back to my back and sigh, almost moaning with the relief of not needing to move again for a while.

One night after tucking each boy into his bed, putting on the sound machine, and walking back to my bed with my third leg crutch, my husband dared to ask the question neither of us wanted to ask. "Babe, what if the surgery gets canceled?" I was brushing my teeth and I said, "I know. I just haven't wanted to say anything," like saying it makes it more possible and ignoring it makes it not a possibility. I stopped and looked at him. God wouldn't do that, right? Like, everything had fallen into place at the eleventh hour. He wouldn't lead me on just for my surgery to be canceled now. Trevor said, "Could you imagine, though? What if it was canceled? What a wild chapter in your future book would that make." I almost laughed at how absurd that idea was as we went to bed, putting that possibility out of our minds again.

I checked my email daily leading up to our departure. Part of me knew . . . it was coming. The other part of me was in straight-up ass shock. *Total shock.*

The dreaded email. I finally got it. The one that said Barcelona had been shut down along with the rest of the world and the hospital was canceling the surgery. I couldn't believe it. I wanted to cry, but I couldn't. Not actually because of the shock but because I felt so much peace in that moment. Like God had come down and held me in His arms while I read the email. My human side was in shock, and my divine side was like, *okay, God's got this. He is faithful.* So I trusted.

I think this blind faith irritated some people around me. It's uncomfortable. *Like, gee, can you tone down your faith to make me more comfortable? I'd feel more comfortable if you whined, or complained, or had a pity party.* Believe me, I am not superhuman. These moments came. I felt them in waves, sometimes lasting days but most of the time lasting just a few hours at a time. I tried to hold space for these emotions but move through them as quickly as possible too.

Like, the faster I got through them the less icky I had to feel. I felt icky enough from the actual physical conditions plaguing this body.

I can look back now, four years later, and be okay with this because I have twenty-twenty vision about it, but at the moment it was brutal. Not knowing was the hardest part. The hospital couldn't give us any timeframe on when the surgery would be rescheduled. The best guess they had was probably fall, and so we were stuck waiting. I felt rush-of-panic moments, like a wave knocking me off my feet and covering my whole body. It was strange, as I was still in paralysis at this point, but I could just feel these waves of heavy fear crash over me, like the outline of my body would appear when they left.

CHAPTER 17

God's Silence

Even though I had faith that was strong as steel, it would sometimes bend and wobble. The times that were the hardest were when I felt as though God was silent.

God's silence—it's deafening.

Don't you agree?

Have you ever experienced the silence of your Almighty Creator and wondered where on this green earth He could possibly be hiding? Like He started a hide-and-go-seek game and you didn't get the memo? Gosh darn it. *Why did I miss that memo?*

God was not only silent after my rape, He was silent many times in my life. Through much of the psychosis I felt for sure if He wasn't going to answer me now, He surely couldn't be this loving Being I originally thought He was. I was so angry at Him then, I actually took a month break from church. I spent those four weeks just letting go of reading the Bible, and I spoke to God with an anger so hot it could burn the sky.

Looking back, it was that anger with God that made me realize I never really stopped believing in His presence at all. *I wouldn't be mad at Him if I didn't believe in Him.*

I felt so alone through part of my paralysis. Why is this happening to me now, God? We were just starting to plan life again, instead of just surviving it. We had JUST sold our house to pay $80,000 for a surgery that got canceled days before we were to leave for Barcelona. I had JUST survived postpartum psychosis and then I became paralyzed. WHERE WAS GOD?

The weeks between when my surgery was canceled and rescheduled God felt so cruel. It was strange: I felt peace and also I felt nothing. Felt comforted and abandoned. Lost in limbo. In the waiting.

I kept wondering, *hey God, could you give me a sneak peek at how long I am going to be tortured in this body? A timeline may help my sanity?*

But there was none given.

I felt His silence as I was up with my son at night when he was a toddler and had night terrors. He'd scream and I couldn't stop it. I would just be with him. I felt God's silence when I had to fight the doctors so damn hard to get my son the proper medical care he needed. A surgery that should have been performed his first year of life was not performed until he was nine. *Why, God?*

I felt the silence as family and friends turned their backs on me because I had left the religion of my upbringing and chosen to just follow God. The God of the Bible. I lost relationships for His true relationship, and then there was still so much silence.

These are just a rainbow of all the times God has been quiet, times that bleed into each other. Like a rainbow, sometimes you can't discern one color from the next, but they are all there. What is so fascinating to me is when God gave me that image for this book, He reminded me of what a rainbow stands for in the Bible: the promise He made to never again flood the earth. He reminds me of the promise He made me when I followed Him and accepted Him in my life: that He will not leave me comfortless, that **He actually lives within me.**

Did you know that God's actual name is Yahweh? The amazing thing about His name is that if you slow down the sound of the human breath, you are proclaiming His name with every breath. He is literally the air that fills your lungs. You breathe Him in all around you and with each breath, your heart beats and pumps blood to all of your body through saying His name.

So, even in the silence, even in the pain, even in the waiting, know that God—*Yahweh*—is with you. He is in every breath you take. He is the love that floods your soul, the oxygen that transfuses your blood. He is the bird in the sky and the clover growing out from under the tree. He is in all of His creations, and you are among one of His most precious ones.

Much like that numb feeling of paralysis—the absence of feeling altogether, the absence of control over my vocal cords—waiting can feel like the absence of guidance, the absence of God. It can feel like suffering, confusion, and grief. Grief for the loss of something we once had or the loss from not feeling like we have been given an answer to the question we are asking.

For me, that question was about healing. The first time was healing my mind and the second was healing my body.

Both limbos, both hurry up and wait. Both experiences left me feeling alone. In those moments I felt like God wasn't showing up for me. In those moments I felt like I was taking one step forward, two steps back . . . or maybe even three or four steps back, never actually getting to where I thought my destination was.

It is those moments I look back on now and see God differently. It is those moments where I see my relationship with God mature, shift, and change. In those moments, looking back I see my shell shatter, my skin shed, and a new me birthed.

To you who look at me now and still struggle to trust that there is hope, still struggle to trust that you aren't utterly alone in this world; to those who still think I am a unicorn—*healing must just be for her, not for me*—know that is not the case.

Know that in your waiting, in your grieving, in your patience a new you is being birthed. Lessons come from this, you just cannot see them now.

In those moments of His silence I learned to SEEK Him more deeply. My ability to rely on my faith was strengthened because it is in the silence that faith is required.

If you feel like Job, and hard things keep happening to you over and over, you are not alone. And if God is silent, keep asking. Keep seeking. Because you will hear Him again. Don't give up.

CHAPTER 18

Purpose in Pain

So often it is hard to see purpose when our sight is clouded with pain. I know what it is like to be blindsided by pain. It can hijack your whole day or even your whole life. It is deafening, blinding, and all-consuming. I have known pain. Endless pain. Pain that seems to have no shape or limits.

I knew pain through postpartum psychosis. I lived with pain during my paralysis, and I experienced pain as I wrote this book, because writing this book made me face the places inside of me I was still ignoring.

On day three of writing this book, a migraine hit me. And I knew . . . this experience was for my book. I was so annoyed. I was so deflated. My reserve for coping with such intense, sharp pain had been worn away the last few weeks with the constant weather changes, and on this exact day, I had nothing left to offer. No grace, no patience, no cheerful outlook. I still did my daily practice of listing out all the things I was grateful for, as this has been a practice I have leaned on every time I am in chronic pain. I know that I can control my thoughts and I cannot let myself spiral, so I count my gratitudes. On this particular day, I shared on my social media all the things I was grateful for.

I'm thankful for healing.

Though not linear or perfect, my quality of life is so much better than I could have ever imagined, and I don't take the good days for granted.

I am grateful for healing my leaky gut.

I am grateful for healing Lyme disease.

I am grateful that my neck has healed enough for me to mostly be out of my neck brace.

I am grateful for technology so I can sit with my camera off on Zoom calls from my tub.

This day, though, the pain would not let up and I knew it was for you. This pain had a purpose.

So I surrendered to it. I let it be. I wanted to write yesterday, but I couldn't look at a screen for most of the day, so I let it be. I wondered, what message do I need to hear through this? And this is what I realized:

I see you.

I FEEL you.

I feel you in every fiber of my being.

Down to my cells, I know you.

I hear the cries of your heart. The heart doesn't need words. Sometimes, words fail us. They don't have enough meaning, especially when it comes to pain.

I have spent many hours in prayers of pure emotions, no words. God doesn't need words. He just knows.

The best gift I can give you, past any words I write, is the gift of being known—truly known and loved.

Your pain does not define you, whether it is physical or emotional. I understand the turmoil of both.

To those who struggle with chronic illness, physical illness, doctor's appointments, families, and the desire to keep going: I see you. I understand the war inside you. *How can I be all I am supposed to be while fighting these battles? I can't ever be enough for them. I don't know how to put one foot in front of the other and yet, each day, I manage to keep living.*

There is a gift here. Many do not know it. Fighting a chronic illness that strips away the life you once knew offers you the opportunity to create a new future, something you may have previously overlooked. You may have jumped into the river of life and just let the current take you wherever it flows. **Now you get to decide.** The river of life tried to drown you. Maybe you still feel like you are under the current, but you will find that though life keeps passing you by, you somehow have become a bystander. You are watching others go past as you are stuck in the shallows.

I have often felt as if I were slowly sinking in quicksand by the side of a river. I was slowly dying, just watching everyone else's lives continue on the river. What I found to be the gift in this is I was given the chance to learn how to BE. *Just be.* Not be a doer. I am a chronic DOER! *Being* has never come easily or naturally to me. And chronic pain led me to understand the power of BEING.

I saw that I still had value. There was value in me even though I could not do the laundry, wash the dishes, or cook the dinner. My presence in my children's and husband's lives was enough.

I was enough.

Yes, someone else had to pick up the slack of the doing I no longer could do, but in the BEING there was magic.

I think I am far too stubborn to learn this lesson any other way. Even yesterday, I was so agitated that I couldn't be productive. I've only been on a true healing journey for two years, yet I've already slipped back into the habit of measuring my worth by how much I accomplish.

I wrestled with my desire to see a list of completed tasks, believing my value depended on those checkmarks. How can I reduce my worth to a list of things I do? How absurd! Yet, this is a battle nearly everyone faces.

We live in a world of chronic busy-ness. I hate when I hear the word *busy* come out of my mouth. When you ask somehow how they *are* and they say "busy" . . . not what you are *doing, how are* you? How is your SOUL? What has made you laugh this week? What has broken your heart? What has made you feel ALIVE?

Can you answer those? Have you slowed down enough to experience life, not just "do" life?

This is the practice: slow down and BE, not do.

I remember a day when I cried in the car on my way to get my blood work done. The story on the radio hit me so hard. I was so grateful for feeling alive by connecting to another human through that story. It slowed me down. It brought me into my body. Connection does that. It takes us from the *doing t*o the **being.**

Doing disconnects us.

Being connects us.

I have found that when I am in the BEING, I am able to connect to my children better. One night as I was tucking my son into bed, I looked my son in the eyes and told him I would move mountains for him. His battles he was facing were big for his young age. He struggled with self-confidence and was lashing out because of it. I wished I could move the mountain he was facing. I wished I could take his pain away, and I desperately needed him to hear that. I honestly was shocked to see his body relax and him maintain eye contact as I continued to tuck him in.

I know that God has felt this same way with me.

I know that many times God has seen me in my pain and wants me to understand the purpose that is held within it.

On one particularly hard day of pain, I felt this message from God:

> *I love you fiercely, and if I could help you understand life doesn't have to be hard, that it may not be easy but it can be enjoyed and even loved, then I would. I need you to know I would move mountains for you. I want you to love life. I want you to find joy in it, and I want you to know even if hard things happen, that doesn't mean life has to be hard. It just means that event sucked and the rest of life is amazing.*
>
> *If I could tell you anything, it is that life doesn't have to be hard. Life can have hard, sucky things in it, but that doesn't mean your whole life is hard. Life was meant to be enjoyed, loved, experienced—not just endured.*
>
> *If I could take your pain from you, I would.*

I can't imagine living in this much pain anymore.

When I am in pain, I just immediately go to gratitude. It isn't even a conscious thing anymore. It is what I do because I can't focus on *what if I live in this much pain everyday.*

Often my pain is a teacher—the teacher of things I am still trying to grasp control over, things I won't let go of. When I ask why I am experiencing the pain, I am surprised to find the answer is given. My body knows. I'll remember an experience that is being repeated in a different way in my present life and my body remembers. It remembers how painful it was to go through last time, and it is doing its best to protect me from facing it again.

Pain can be a great teacher. It can help us learn to care for ourselves, it can teach us to have compassion for others, and it can lead us to ultimate healing. We just have to stop running from it.

What would happen for you if you looked at your pain as a teacher, or even a healer, cleansing you from the inside? How would that shift and change you?

CHAPTER 19

Comparison

Throughout my chronic illness journey, I often found myself falling into comparison. Most of the time it was my default setting, though I wasn't even aware comparison *was* my default setting.

I thought I had made great progress with my mindset through therapy during postpartum psychosis, but maybe I hadn't fully worked on this area yet.

Pain is often the result of comparison: comparing what we *think* we should feel or be to what is actually happening. Comparison is the seed of suffering. You might find comparison is your default setting. It's okay, it is what we are taught growing up. Often in public schools we find ourselves comparing our grades to others, our learning speed to our neighbors', our reading score to our friends'. This becomes our default coding, and it can lead to great suffering as adults.

When we fall into comparison, we are taken into a lack mindset where there is not enough. Enough space for each of us to be uniquely us. That what we have to say was already said or taught. That who we are doesn't have a place in this world.

Now, in this era of social media, teen suicide rates are higher than ever before and are even starting in children younger than I even dared to imagine. We are losing ten year olds to suicide. Comparison leads to death. While it might not result in physical death for everyone, it can cause spiritual and emotional death. It kills our uniqueness—what makes us so special and beautiful in God's eyes.

We scroll social media and see how we aren't pretty enough, smart enough, special enough to get likes, views, or comments. We lack the confidence and self-love to own who we are and know that we are enough just as we are. *You are loved and precious and God did not make a mistake when He made you.*

I would find myself on Facebook support groups and hear other people's stories. I would compare where I was to those stories. I would compare the pain I had to theirs. I would compare how crippled they were to me. After my surgery, I would fall victim to comparing healing. Why was theirs more straightforward, why is mine such a rollercoaster? All the comparing can only lead to suffering. Even in the highs of my recovery going well, comparison led to suffering because it gave me survivor's guilt, especially when I compared myself to close friends who were in the lows of recovery while I was experiencing a moment of high in my recovery. The guilt would eat me alive, and I hated it. Then I would punish myself for thinking like this and feel guilty for things working for me. The highs would never last with the victim mindset and the survivor's guilt. With time a flare would rear its ugly head and I would slip into the suffering of going through my own low.

I often look back on this experience in my life and see that it was just a season. I had more hard things in front of me, but I compared my good times to those friends who were still in the muck. Rather than letting myself be a roadmap for them, I got stuck in guilt and judgment. Instead, embrace the now with grace and love and appreciation because you never know what tomorrow holds.

I also fell into the trap of the comparison mindset in motherhood. Many mothers do. Whenever I talk about my postpartum psychosis, I actually lead with the suggestion, "Do not compare your journey to mine because as soon as you compare your postpartum to my extreme postpartum, you'll belittle your own experience. You'll mainly think, 'Mine wasn't that bad, so I shouldn't be complaining. I can get myself out of this because I wasn't the same extreme.'" I hear this in motherhood. I hear this when I share my experience with chronic illness, like, "Wow, you've gone through so much! I shouldn't complain. I've just been going through XYZ."

People compare the healing journeys of others who've had similar surgeries as I or have the same genetic conditions and then they think,

"Oh, she's had it worse," or "I don't know how she does it with four kids. I couldn't do it with children." When you fall into comparison, it's like you are building your own prison walls. It's like locking the chain and throwing away the key. What you're really doing is judging yourself, and you can never heal from a place of judgment. Judgment and love don't coincide. Let others' journeys be roadmaps or markers on the trail. Let them offer guidance, affirmation that you're on the right path and even in the right community, but don't let their journeys keep you stuck.

People often only share parts of their lives, so you never truly know someone else's full story. Yet, we tend to judge everything about ourselves—our good days, bad days, ugly moments, and not-so-awesome days—based on those incomplete glimpses of others. You only see these snippets of someone else's life, and you fall into comparison and self-judgment, but you really don't know their life, and they really don't know yours, and you have no clue what's in front of you.

Comparison is the seed of all illness. It will plague, destroy, and paralyze you so that you can't see your dreams. There is so much ahead of you if only you will stop looking to others and look within. Let go without judgment so you can embrace and trust the path you are on.

CHAPTER 20

Grief of the Should-Have-Beens . . .

There have been so many times when grief has struck me unexpectedly. It seems to come out of nowhere, just when I thought I was doing fine. *Grief, why did you have to show yourself again? I thought I had you tamed and under control.* . . . It erupts unexpectedly.

Grief is unpredictable and relentless, refusing to stay hidden for long. Just when I believe I've managed to keep it at bay, it resurfaces, reminding me of its presence. It's like trying to tame a wild animal that always finds a way to break free. This constant battle with grief feels never-ending, and just when I think I've mastered it, it catches me off guard once more.

There were many times after my fourth son was born that I wished I could reverse time. I longed to return to a specific moment when it was just the three boys and me: a day trip to Heber and Midway, Utah. I remember that near the end of the day, all of the boys were running around the park where the grass was so green, and they were all finding immense joy in simply playing on the bleachers set up for soccer games. Trevor was playing with them, and I took a photograph that has both haunted and fueled me over the years.

It has haunted me because I desperately wanted to go back and experience that day again. Go back to just three kids. I loved how they found joy in such simple things.

It has fueled me because I knew if I found such simple love, joy, and gratitude for motherhood once, *I knew I could do it again.*

I reflect on this moment because it seems to be the first in a broken record that began to play in my head. I began to grieve things I thought my chronic illness had taken away from me for good.

The "should nots" that accompany my illness.

It seemed that wherever I turned, I was given a list of things I "should not" do.

"Brooke, you are fused, you should not ride rollercoasters." *That's fine, Doc, no argument from me.*

"You should not ride a four-wheeler, go snowmobiling, boating, or ever ride horses again. Brooke, you should not do anything with harsh impact."

GRIEF OF THE SHOULD-HAVE-BEENS . . .

I took some of these suggestions like they were commandments from God rather than guidelines. I mourned the prognosis, yet, I was filled with so much gratitude for what I did have again in my life: feeling in my body, temperature gauge on my skin and in my mouth, the feeling of texture beneath my feet, the release of a migraine that had lasted ten months straight. Every day I woke up after my surgery, I found more I had regained. I was walking independently, without crutches within three days of having my head cut open.

At first, the cost of regaining all these abilities seemed insignificant. I wasn't even sad when the doctor told me the things I should *not* do because I had already gained so much back, with even more to come. I could cook for my family again, drive, run errands, grocery shop, and take my kids to school—all the things I had mourned for so long.

Over the years, I experienced several flares that would completely incapacitate me. For example, a double pelvis dislocation once put me in bed for an entire week. I was in excruciating pain. The dislocation also misaligned my spine, resulting in vertigo. I couldn't bear weight on my legs, and my husband had to carry me to the bathroom, pull down my pants, put me on the toilet, and then reverse the process to get me back to bed. I would cry in anguish and sometimes curse at God, questioning where He was in all of this.

During these times, I remembered my teenage years as an equestrian vaulter when I felt the freedom of moving my body to music as I danced on top of a horse. It had saved me as a teenager after my rape and other significant losses. During those dark moments as an adult, I mourned my healthy body, feeling as if I would never experience good health again.

In those dark times, it was easy to forget how big God is and to believe the lies my mind and the devil told me: that this suffering would never end and that it was my new normal. I grieved all the things that *should have been*.

I would grieve the miles I *could have* run in the last few years, the horses I *should have* sat upon, my boys' activities I had missed—the games I didn't have the ability to focus on to play with them. I grieved it all like multiple deaths.

Every time I grieved these losses I would have to then flip that mourning and let it act as resurrection fire within me. It would add lighter fluid to the fire of my determination to heal to regain those activities.

I chose to live beyond the prognosis the doctor gave me. I believed that I would still be able to live, and live fully. Even with a fusion, EDS, MCAS, and Lyme disease. Even with chronic illness. **I chose to live.**

I have now purchased my new pair of running shoes. With the progress in my healing, my surgeon has approved me picking up running again because I have been a long-distance runner since I was ten. Since writing my first draft of this book I have begun to run again! It was like no time had passed, even though it had been four-and-a-half years since I had run. Every time I regain an ability to do something, the same freedom I felt in my chest all those years ago riding horses rises up again in my belly and I feel the power I hold within me. **The power to live a full life**, *even with!*

A few weeks ago, a doctor asked if I ever wanted to ride a horse again. My heart leapt out of my chest. He said he felt like if I went on a horse that was trained well enough to teach kids to ride, that would be all right because of my healing!

I have ridden four-wheelers with my children and husband. I have sat and putted around the meadow on a snowmobile and watched my children's free spirits let loose in the fields as they've learned to drive those snow scoots.

You do not need to lose something to not take it for granted. Don't take for granted the moments, the activities that light your soul on fire. Every time you do one, take a moment to pause and actually soak it in, like enjoying all the flavors life has to offer you. This is the feeling of really living and not just surviving.

CHAPTER 21

Prognosis Power

A prognosis only has the power you give it. Why do you think people die the exact day the doctor predicted? The doctor is not God. He did not predict the death day. He gave his prediction, and the person bought into it with their whole soul.

I should be paralyzed right now.

But I am not.

I should be in a wheelchair.

But I am not.

I shouldn't be writing this book.

But I am.

I shouldn't be Lyme-free.

But I am.

I decided to believe a different story.

Who said I can't heal? Who said you can't heal?

When I realized I was giving away so much of my power, I was a bit shocked. I couldn't believe this bold, self-disciplined, determined lady had bought into those stories. *Then again, I can.*

I remember the day I sat in the doctor's office getting my certificate for a disability license plate for my car. My doctor was filling out the paperwork for me to get an official plate on my car, not just the paper that hangs in the window (that had already expired). I remember sitting on the chair and wondering . . . *how did my life come to this point? How could I have gone from being an active, healthy mother on the playground with her four boys to one who can't even always take care of herself?*

I always imagined I'd be putting a marathon sticker on my back windshield, not switching out my license plates to replace them with disability plates. It was in moments like this that, for a minute, I absorbed the weight of how poor my health really was. The rest of the time I was so focused on surviving that I wouldn't allow myself to experience the emotional pain of my present day.

After all, I was walking a road not many had walked and there were no trail markers for me.

Let this book, and especially this chapter, be a guidepost for you on your walk of life. Let me remind you that all you have to do is reclaim your power and your voice. All you have to do is decide *that narrative* doesn't fit your story.

This does not mean your diagnosis was incorrect. By gosh, mine were spot on. I mean, I have bloodwork, imaging, and genetic testing that shows the reality of them all. It just means I did not give away my power forever. I fell prey to believing it for a time. I am human, *as are you.* **But, I always remember who I am, and I take back the power within myself.**

I will always remember the day I took my power back. It had been a long journey. Between my battle with postpartum psychosis, suicidal ideation, chronic illness, a skull-cervical fusion, paralysis, and all of the struggles in between, I had fully given my power over to my circumstances. Then, one day, two-and-a-half years ago, I dragged my tired body into a hot CBD bath to ease the pain that was pulsing through me like a heartbeat. The throbbing in my head was excruciating, and my body felt like it was taped together with the braces I wore for stability. Over the next few hours the hot water dissolved the pain and my mind cleared. It was in these moments that I felt my soul begging for the next answer when this solution hit me like a ton of bricks. I saw a truth that made me cringe. I wanted to ignore it. I wanted to delete it, but I couldn't. It was here, and the truth doesn't run away. It stands there looking at us square in the face.

I saw that I had made chronic illness my identity. I saw that my chronic illness had become my badge of honor.

When this truth was shown to me, the other truth appeared. And it came in the form of a question . . . *Who said I can't heal?*

After all, I have managed to accomplish a lot, even with chronic illness. If I could do all that, surely I could conquer the mind and find healing. I knew that my biggest obstacle would be the belief. Once I honestly believed I could heal, I knew my body would follow.

Somehow, conquering the mind in this way seemed far scarier than facing suicidal ideation had been. I could take medication to help manage my symptoms as I worked on building my mental strength to stabilize my life again. However, there was no medication to give me courage, faith, or hope.

Those are all very vulnerable feelings when you have lived in the prison of chronic illness. Allowing yourself to feel any of those emotions seems almost scarier than staying stuck in the illness forever. Do you know why? **Because being stuck is familiar.** *Healing is unfamiliar.* Healing is scary; it is risky to take a chance on yourself. It defies everything the medical system tells us nowadays. The truth is, your mind holds the power that either keeps you stuck or unlocks the gates to healing.

In the next chapter I am going to get so real with you and show you some of the processes I have used to find healing. There is not just one way to heal. There is not a one-size-fits-all approach, so do not get yourself stuck because you want healing to be spelled out for you. Instead, let the variety of ways to find healing be freeing to your soul. Approach healing with the lighthearted spirit of play and not the desperation of "if this doesn't work, then it is hopeless." The latter is what will feel most like a default setting. It will take practice to approach healing with the perception of play, lightheartedness, and hope. I know that feels strange to read together. Play and healing practices . . . I can hear you saying to me, "Brooke, you don't understand. I lie in bed all day. I can't play."

I know. I was there once too. Let me tell you, your heart needs this. It needs light heartedness, the safety that brings to your nervous system. It needs you to take the pressure off of it because you won't find healing if you are pressuring it to come. As long as there is pressure, the prognosis holds the power. The nervous system is in fight-or-freeze, and you can't heal in that state.

My invitation to you is to sit with these two questions:

> *Where were you when you bought into chronic illness as your identity?*
>
> *Did you realize you had done so?*

Allow yourself to go into the next chapter with an open mind and open heart and see what God speaks to you through it. Writing this next chapter was one of the hardest to write in this book. I worked through some of my chronic illness baggage in real time as I was writing this section. I hope you take the time to do the steps in the next chapter with me.

CHAPTER 22

Chronic Illness Identity

The biggest breakthrough in my healing was when I became aware I had the *identity* of chronic illness, and I didn't even realize I did. When I put a name to it, I felt the weight of that badge of honor, and as the truth settled over me, I was finally able to lay it down.

I know this topic is going to be hard to digest. Please don't run away from this. I know it is uncomfortable. I know the pain that lives within this truth. But I promise, you deserve a life without this chronic illness. And so, I am inviting you to stay with me here. Sit in the uncomfortable to GET to where you are meant to be: a life of joy, freedom, and peace. A life of health.

As we venture through this chapter, take time to journal whenever it gets uncomfortable. Let yourself FEEL and then release into the new future as you let go of the pain that has been holding you in a dungeon, a prisoner of pain and fear. So lean in and I will walk beside you each step of the way.

Chronic illness is the worst. It steals your joy and can fill you with bitterness and frustration. But, there's a secret hidden within the layers of chronic illness. And this secret is going to be the thing that frees you.

To uncover this secret, I am going to ask you questions. I invite you to answer below where I have created space for you to work through this.

How are you *benefiting* from your chronic illness?

I know.

I know.

That question is weird.

But sit with me for a minute. I want you to think about this.

Are you getting out of family parties, bedtime routines with the children, running the errands, doing the dishes, taking out the trash because of your chronic illness? Is it allowing you to hide, to disconnect from the world, to be alone more? The danger of being alone is that is when the enemy can strike. When we are alone we have no one to speak truth to us, and it is easy for us to believe the lies the devil tells us. So ask the hard question: what has chronic illness given you?

For many who have dealt with chronic illness, it has fully taken over their identity. Everyone knows about your illness. They know that you need to rest more, you can't help out much, and many won't expect a lot from you.

This is a benefit that someone gets when they allow chronic illness to own them.

It's like a get-out-jail-free card.

And we hold it like a badge of honor at the same time.

So . . . yes, your chronic illness IS benefiting you, which allows your body to hold onto it longer.

The next question is going to tip the tables for you. And I want you to really focus on this one:

What has your chronic illness *taken* from you?

It has stolen time, taken away potential memories with loved ones, made you miss conversations around the fire pit and mundane dancing in the kitchen. It has come in like a thief and stolen precious moments in the carpool lane at after-school pick up when your kids just needed to hear their parent's voice. Either they have really exciting news or they had a really bad day and a parent should be the first one to greet them. Holding the badge of chronic illness has taken this from you because you're holding this badge so white-knuckled that you can't catch anything else until you're willing to pry your fingers away and drop it. There is no room in your life to be who you were meant to be. Chronic illness has deleted parts of your life that you can never get back.

But there is still the NOW and the future ahead. It IS possible to live without chronic illness. And it all begins with living into a new story for ourselves.

Now dream with me.

What would your life be without your chronic illness? What's the first thing you would do? Would you plan a trip, read a book, drive your kids to school? What are the mundane things that you are missing out on that are really full of magic? Our life is made up of the magic of the small, mundane things each day. It's where we shape who we are, who our children are going to be, what our family culture will be. What have you been missing out on?

I know it sounds hard, but the first step is to be willing to let go of that badge of honor. This badge is so easy to hide behind. It's the comfort that you live in. I know pain is not comfortable, but it is all you know right now, so it is comfortable, familiar. You know what to expect, and it is the same day in and day out. Letting go of it is unfamiliar, and unfamiliar does not equal safety to the nervous system. So, letting go of your chronic illness badge will create stress for you. At first it will feel like panic, like the world is falling out from below your feet. The silence where the pain once was will feel like drowning.

What do you do with the silence?

That is where the magic of choice comes in, the magic of creating the life you were always meant to live instead of living a life governed by your chronic illness. Living without chronic illness feels fearless to me. But then, what is "fearless"? Fearless is scary because you have no fences, you have no ceiling, you have no cap. There's no sky pushing down on you. It is fully stepping into the power of *who you are* and *who God called you to be*. You will never step into healing as long as you hold the badge of honor.

I am inviting you to let it go.

Lay it down.

And I am right here beside you.

I want you to close your eyes and see the chronic illness badge in your hand; it's gold, cold, distant. The way your hands fit around it you feel the sharp edges as your fingers mold around the badge; it's uncomfortable to hold. It's heavy. Now, one-by-one, open your fingers until you release your grip. See it sitting in your hand and then turn your hand upside down. Like it's a ball, watch it land at your feet and bounce. Draw your attention back to your hand. Can you believe how much weight you were holding, how heavy that was? Your fingers cramp; they need to stretch. Moving your fingers after so long feels uncomfortable, but your brain knows your fingers were meant to move. Your nervous system wants to keep them stuck closed. You are going to have to tell your nervous system that it is okay to let go. Embrace your nervous system with so much love and gratitude—it thinks it's been keeping you safe. Thank your nervous system for doing its job.

Honor it and let it know that now you know better and that you are taking the reins back.

Now, you are stepping into a new program, a new way of thinking, a new way of living, and you honor your nervous system for bringing you to who you are today. But that way of living no longer serves you, and that's okay. Do this with so much love and gratitude, not anger, not resentment, not frustration or judgment for how many years you may have been dealing with chronic illness. Thank the illness for the journey. That is what life is—it's the journey, not a destination. You're not going to magically be healed with a snap of your fingers. Even when you have reached healed status, whatever that is for you, you're still on a journey of growing and healing.

I believe that chronic illness is here to teach us something. And if we learn to listen to our body, the wisdom within us will guide us. All you need to do is ask and then listen. There is the deep truth that lives at the center of your chronic illness, but that's not usually what we hear. Instead, we hear the noise of it, always running on a loop within us.

Right now, chronic illness has you on speed dial, and it is going to keep calling and calling. Eventually you're going to get tired of ignoring it and you're going to think, *if I just answer, then it will stop calling.* And that is when slippery fingers grasp you once again and pull you back in. Don't be ashamed when this happens because growth is not linear. Much like a roller coaster, there will be some twists and turns and maybe loop-de-loops. It's okay if you give in and answer. Don't judge yourself for it; just recognize it, learn from it, and grow from it. Each time your chronic illness calls, you will become stronger until it's like you put chronic illness on "do not disturb" and it will not come through anymore, and eventually it stops calling. There's no room for it in your life anymore because you have outgrown what it has taught you.

I know that chronic illness feels like a security blanket, but don't be fooled. It's a lie. It's a security blanket that will become a straitjacket. It is your choice to stay in the straitjacket or unlatch it. I know it doesn't feel like you have a choice when you're in the straitjacket; how am I supposed to unlatch a straitjacket? I know that doesn't make sense and is completely illogical. And that's the power—the fact that you *do* have a choice. The straitjacket is trying to lie to you to make you believe that it has the power over you when, in fact, you have the power over the straitjacket. It is not a security blanket. It is keeping you stuck in the suffering, in the pain, in the loneliness, in all the things that you wish you weren't dealing with.

I hate the term "victim" in my chronic illness because I understand my power, and the pain I experienced from chronic illness is truly my last hurdle in claiming the stage I am in. I am *not* a victim. I know this and yet, even though I don't believe I'm a victim, I still *feel* like a victim to these migraines that control my life. I feel like I can't plan, I can't predict because I don't know when they'll hit. I have had to put off planning family vacation because we never know when these migraines will come. I have put off speaking on stages because I never know when the pain will show up. My chronic illness has jumped into the driver's seat of my car in this life.

I am currently writing this book with a migraine. My head throbs, my neck feels like an earthquake, and I think there's a bomb going off in my left eye. I have prayed all day that God would just take this from me because I am writing this book that He has called me to write. Why isn't He taking it? I know He can and that's what's so frustrating. I know it's so easy to read this chapter and say, "I call bullshit," to dismiss what I have to say, but I can only boldly write these words on this page because I live it and you can't be told by an outsider how to heal. You have to know that I walk in this rut with you, that I am in the trenches, and that is why I can boldly and almost harshly call *bullshit* on the belief that chronic illness is in charge.

> We need to live differently.
> We need to live differently.
> We need to live differently.
> *You* need to live differently.

People are catering to you. They are walking on eggshells. I know that hurts to hear, but it is the truth. I want to invite you into a process that changed my life. I want you to look at your chronic illness. How is it benefiting you? On this first part of the table you are going to write all the ways it is benefiting you. On the other part of the table you are going to write all the things it has cost you. I know many of you are going to be tempted to jump over this.

DON'T.

To help you get started I am going to share my table with you. I am going to share the one I just made about my migraines.

What are the benefits of having migraines?

- Hide from my kids in overwhelm.
- Lie in a dark room.
- Listen to my favorite show.
- Take a bath.
- I don't have to make dinner.
- I don't have to be a taxi driver.
- I don't have to clean the house.
- It's an excuse not to claim my power.
- It's an excuse to be a loner.

What does a migraine cost me?

- It costs me precious moments with my boys that I won't get back.
- It costs my husband, makes him my caregiver and shifts our relationship.

- It costs me my voice, my power.
- It costs me connection and community.
- It costs me stages, podcasts, and running retreats that will save lives.

Releasing the Chronic Illness Badge

What are the benefits of having (insert your chronic illness here)

- _____
- _____
- _____
- _____
- _____
- _____

What does my chronic illness cost me?

- _____
- _____
- _____
- _____
- _____

The cost runs deeper than the benefits.

When you look at the benefits of my migraines, you may notice the same pattern I noticed. It all revolves around: I won't give myself permission to rest or do something for me when I need to. You know what my body has to say about that?

You won't claim permission, so I am going to force you to stop.

The shift I need to make is claiming my voice: asking for help with running the kids to sports, asking for someone else to do the dishes or make the food, telling my children I need ten minutes alone, telling them I am taking a bath and I'll be back.

In the culture I was raised in, mothers self-sacrifice to their death. The examples I dominantly had surrounding me did not show how to ask for what you need. They showed how to wait until someone gives you permission to stop, like, "Good job, gold star, now you've earned a fifteen-minute break." **NO!** Eff that shit! I am reclaiming my power. I am claiming my voice.

Imagine the gift I am teaching my children to claim: to serve from a full cup and not out of obligation or resentment (which comes from serving from an empty cup). Imagine what I am teaching them when I firmly, boldly state what I need and then claim it. Imagine the life partner they will each attract into their lives because they were taught this skill when they were children.

Look back at your table. What are the themes you see there?

> **Use the space below to write out each of the themes. Break the power they have over you by writing them down here.**
>
> _____
> _____
> _____
> _____
> _____
> _____
> _____
> _____
> _____
> _____
> _____
> _____
> _____
> _____
> _____
> _____

What do you need to do to shift these beliefs?

For me, it is as simple as asking for help. I'm terrible at it. I'm terrible at vocalizing my needs. I can imply them, I can beat around the bush, but for a bold woman it sure seems strange that I can't state some of my most basic human needs.

Write below the shift that needs to take place for your beliefs' themes to change.

What is the first action step you can take to make this shift in your life?

For me, it will be sitting down with my husband, sharing what I have learned about myself, and discussing specific ways he can help me to not feel like I am carrying the load in the places I saw the benefits to my migraines. It will be about setting healthy boundaries with my children. Just because I am their mom, that does not mean they need 24-7 access to me. For a very long time I believed my children should have unlimited access to me because, having been raised by divorced parents, I did not have access to my mom whenever I wanted. My children will know that once I have refilled my cup, I can be fully present with them and they will appreciate the authentic connection I am able to provide from a full cup.

Lean into the growth this is allowing you. Lean into doing it imperfectly, and use the pain as a reminder that you may have gotten offtrack in your healing journey. Remember that chronic illness has you on speed dial; do not judge yourself when it comes calling. Hit the red "ignore" button without sending the call to voicemail. You have control here. YOU have unbuckled the shackles of your straitjacket and are reclaiming your life. Only you have that power!

You need to know that I still experience the calling of chronic illness even years into healing. Healing is not a race. You didn't break overnight, and you won't heal overnight, either. I am here in these trenches with you. I am laying my skeletons out there for you to know I am doing the work too. So, I have to share this next part with you.

I'm in the process of editing this book and I was hit by another wild migraine. It's been a few weeks since I have had one that has taken me out—since I wrote the beginning of this chapter. I found myself so frustrated that chronic illness was calling me again, just as I told you it does.

I made it through my morning obligation and then lay down in my bed, head covered, too nauseous to even take a bath to help the pain, and I thought of you. I thought, *am I sharing something in this book that I shouldn't?* For a moment, I let doubt set in. For a time, I debated about editing this chapter. And then my answer was *in* this chapter. I had already written to myself as a reminder of all I have been through in my healing journey. That is, sometimes chronic illness comes calling and we have to be strong enough to put it on do not disturb.

Then I felt confused because I have practiced owning my voice, taking breaks, and caring for my nervous system throughout the day, so I knew this headache was not from failing to do that. I spent much of the day feeling like I was asking the wrong question about my headache. Finally, the nausea eased up enough for a bath and as I slid into the water, I changed the question I was asking. I asked, "What is my body remembering?"

Boom!

I hit the nail on the head. My body was remembering a trauma. You see, in the thick of my postpartum psychosis, just a few weeks before I was hospitalized, I made the dumb decision of being too selfless and agreeing that Trevor should go on a three-day work trip he had scheduled. Those three days were honestly hell. Not just from the psychosis, but I had three kids choke on the same dinner in one night and I had to do the Heimlich on each of them.

That was the last time Trevor has left me home with the kids. For over five years, I haven't been left with them—not because I was mentally incapable but because of my physical illness. Whenever we've been away from the kids, it has been for medical reasons, such as my surgery in Barcelona or my trips to Mexico for Lyme disease treatments.

So, this migraine I got while editing my book hit the day before Trevor was to leave for three days. The crazy part is, my conscious mind had no problem with him leaving. I was happy for him to get out of the house, see friends, and get a break from his routine for a few days. I was happy to be the one staying home and supporting our kids during their last week of school. My body, my nervous system, though, had a different perspective. My nervous system just remembered how terribly wrong everything had gone last time he was gone. How my mental health had been literally wrestling with the devil, and how I had almost lost three of our kids in one night. Of course my nervous system sirens were going off! Red lights flashing and all. As soon as I asked my body what it was remembering, and why it was experiencing the migraine, I was shocked at the response.

My conscious mind had not connected the two events. I had not realized that was the last time Trevor had left me home with the kids. My body knew, though, and it was in full panic mode. As soon as I acknowledged the trauma my body was holding, thanked it for alerting me, and reminded my nervous system we have a new program we are running, my pain began to go away. I am honestly almost shocked. *Within two hours of recognizing the root of my pain, I was pain free again.*

Revisiting the last time Trevor left us wasn't comfortable, but I know I'm not in that place anymore. I felt confident in supporting him being away for a few days. Honestly, I'm just so impressed with our bodies; they're programmed to keep us safe and communicate with us in any way they can. Unfortunately for me, that communication comes through migraines.

How is your body communicating with you? Is it as simple as not asking the right question or needing to reword your question to figure out why you are experiencing the symptoms that plague you?

I know this chapter might rattle you, but let it. Read it a few times if you need to.

Why?

Because if you can fully embrace the truth in this chapter, you will be on the path to freedom.

And you deserve to be free from the prison of chronic illness.

CHAPTER 23

The Ultimate Betrayal

As I have experienced hours of therapy, a mental hospital stay, medical facilities, and being alone with my thoughts, I have found the one single thread that ties all of these traumas together.

And when I saw it, I wanted to ignore it. I wanted to forget it. Not believe it, hide it, and delete it. Because the shame of this conversation is too heavy.

When I first became aware of it, I didn't believe it. I pushed it to the side and thought, *of course I trust my body.*

The truth is, I didn't trust my body. This body, MY body, reacted to the rape, and so I made a decision at that moment that I could never trust my body again.

My body had betrayed me.

And that belief was sewn into my DNA and my body would continue to be a place of distrust for the next fifteen years.

THE ULTIMATE BETRAYAL

The rape is where it all began, but I only just saw it for the first time.

This was the source of my distrust with my body.

When I miscarried my first baby, I felt like I couldn't trust my body.

When I couldn't produce enough breastmilk for my firstborn, I felt like I couldn't trust my body.

When I had postpartum anxiety after birthing my second child, I felt like I couldn't trust my body.

When I had sex with my husband, I felt like I couldn't trust my body not to haunt me with flashbacks and pain.

When I had postpartum psychosis after birthing my fourth son, I felt like I couldn't trust my body.

When I gained weight and couldn't lose it, of course . . . I can't trust my body to do even that.

When I ended up in the hospital in paralysis, unable to even speak—all I could do was blink—I knew I couldn't trust my body.

When my fusion only half-fused, I wasn't surprised. Of course it did. I could not trust my body.

When my body reacted to assault, I chose to believe that I couldn't trust my body.

Now it is obvious. This pattern of belief was reinforced over and over. This distrust was keeping me stuck, **and stagnancy leads to illness.**

Did you know that one out of four women and one out of twenty-six men in a room have been sexually abused? In addition, 53% of woman and 29% of men report experiencing some form of sexual violence.[2] And those are just the cases that were reported to the authorities. Most, like mine, are never shared. So, the numbers are larger than we want to believe. It is very likely that you, reading this book, may have also been through such horrific trauma.

I want to talk to you about how the body works. It is similar to a machine or the electricity in your house. If you flip the switch on for the light, the light turns on.

No one ever makes that mean anything.

The body is the same, **but we shame it.**

We judge ourselves! This judgment does not serve us.

If you are sexually assaulted, the body doesn't register it as assault; it just turns on the machinery.

And so it is very likely that if you were raped or sexually abused, your body reacted to the abuse, simply because that is the machinery of the body.

---

[2] "How Common Is Sexual Assault? Look at These Statistics," by Charlie Health Editorial Team, clinically reviewed by Dr. Don Gasparini, *Charlie Health*, March 29, 2024, https://www.charliehealth.com/post/sexual-assault-statistics.

But we shame ourselves.

There is shame if the person being assaulted feels pleasure during the assault.

And that shame leads to one thing . . . **a distrust in one's own body.**

This chapter is here to show you the truth. I want to help you draw a straight line between the lies that have been filling your head—that have ultimately led you to distrust your body—and the truths that have been hidden from your sight and mind.

LIES:

> Because I reacted, I must've liked it.
>
> If my body reacted, then I must've caused it.
>
> If my body reacted, then I am bad, dirty, not worthy of love or happiness.
>
> If my body reacted, then I am broken.

TRUTHS:

My body reacted because that is the physical mechanism of my body.

> Even though my body reacted:
>
> I did not like it;
>
> I did not cause it;

I did not enjoy it;

I did not ask for it.

I am not dirty, evil, used, or devalued.

The distrust magnifies everything.

The body is our most concrete reality. We could have everyone in the world leave us, and all we would be left with is our body.

So what happens when that ONE thing, the ONE place that never leaves us, feels as though it betrays us?

This is the ultimate loss.

So when we feel like the body betrayed us . . . our trust is destroyed—our trust in ourselves.

This can show up as health problems, relationship problems, money problems, or even business problems.

For me, it showed up in my health problems. It showed up in my relationship with money. It showed up in my motherhood journey. I had to work so hard to find my way back to myself, to learn to trust myself. In this process I realized I was not 100% better because I had not yet come back to trusting my body.

This breakthrough feels so huge, heavy, icky, thick as mud—and on the other side, like complete freedom. It feels like gratitude for the breath in my lungs. It feels like the sun dancing on my skin, charging my soul like a battery. It feels like yearning to be with my husband because it's not uncomfortable to my skin to enjoy intimacy anymore, because this body ... this body *is mine*. It works exactly as God created it to work. It has grown babies, it has supported me through surgeries, it has held my spirit when broken *and* whole, it gives me the ability to experience this life in the flesh. It contains my spirit to this realm as much as gravity holds me down. This body allows me to feel the lows and the highs; without those lows, my highs would not be so sweet.

I have spent the last twelve months regaining trust in my body and it shows in my healing of my chronic illness. I have made quantum leaps in healing throughout the last year, and it is because I am on a learning journey to trust and feel safe in my body again.

I want to provide a place for you to journal at the end of this chapter if this message has impacted you. If you relate to distrusting your body, let's work through the emotions right now.

If you need some guidance to get started, start by listing how this distrust has shown up in your life. Bringing awareness to it without judgment is the first step of healing. Then, thank your body for all the ways it has shown up for you, *even through your distrust*. Write out all the things your body has done right, and show grace to yourself for the judgment you have carried this far. It is time to realize you and your body are on the same team and that it is through this body you get to experience all the beautiful things this life has to offer.

I always include gratitude. Show gratitude for all those things you just listed that your body has done right for you and let it be the start of the new relationship as a team with your body.

One of the last things I do, that you can do, too, is imagine a beautiful healing light from heaven coming through the crown of my head, inhaling through my nose, and seeing this light touch each part of my body from head to toe. As the light reaches each part of your body, welcome it back home and reclaim this body part as yours. It is working for you and with you, not against you. Exhale all that does not serve you anymore—all the judgment, the distrust—and let it feed the earth. Let Mother Earth receive that and bury it for you. You just receive the healing light and start anew.

A Journal Holds No Judgment

A Journal Holds No Judgment

CHAPTER 24

Healing is Written in Your Cells

At a cellular level your body wants to heal. OH it is beautiful. Magical and miraculous. Our bodies are designed to heal from the inside out. Even the biggest bone in the body only takes six to eight weeks to heal fully. *Can you believe that?* What I found in my own healing journey, both physical and mental, was that my brain was the only thing stopping me from healing. *Ugh, my brain!* It has good intentions. The brain's ego is there to keep us safe. The constant thoughts of worst-case scenarios are meant to keep us out of danger, but what they are really doing is keeping us stuck in that loop. Stuck in our *Groundhog Day*—the same day repeated over and over again.

For healing, you have to get out of your head and get into your heart. Not your human heart, your divine heart. Much like the heart keeps your body alive, you have a spiritual heart that keeps your spirit alive, the bridge connecting us to the Divine—to God. This is where our hearts bridge the two worlds: this earth—fully human side—and the heavens—fully divine side. Where God enters in and our bodies work perfectly, as they are supposed to. We experience pain in this mortal world. We experience brokenness, abuse, tragedies, heartache, loss, grief, fire, floods—all these mortal, broken experiences—things that make you wonder where God really is in all of it. Then there is the divine heart that connects us to our higher self, our truest self. The one that your cells listen to, and when this heart speaks, they listen. They heal, they move.

I used to feel broken on a cellular level, like God made a mistake with me. One of my chronic conditions is a genetic degenerative disorder called Ehlers-Danlos Syndrome. There was a time after my surgery when I thought God had made a mistake with me. *That I was a mistake.* He spoke to me in those moments and told me I was not a mistake. But more than that, He told me I was threaded together in my mother's womb. Each part of me, from my hair color to my DNA sequence, was purposeful and I was no mistake! **God does not make mistakes.** How crazy of me to even question that! I heard clearly that I wasn't broken, and then a song came to my mind. A Christian artist sings of a tapestry and the back is a mess. The threads don't make sense, they are tangled, knots everywhere, and there seems to be no order to the chaos. Then you flip it over and, WOW. Breathtaking! You see this beautiful needlework, the threads in designs that you can't see from the backside. So are we. We only see the back of the canvas. It is not until later, sometimes years later, that we can see the needlework being made.

Remember, you are not a mistake. Oh, don't let the devil win with that lie! When you hear that, stop it right there. Do not let it spiral. Do not let it go any further. It is a lie. You only speak the truth to yourself. You are beautifully and wonderfully made. Each part of you is precious and as unique as each snowflake or each fingerprint. There will neve be another one just like you. That is your power.

So if healing is written in your cells, and if your body can heal a broken bone in just a few weeks without you consciously thinking about it, why are you still sick?

My belief is that your subconscious mind and body are fighting. Your body is saying "we can heal," and your subconscious mind is stuck in the negative loop of illness. The way to reprogram the subconscious brain is to rewire the conscious brain.

How do we do that? I think the easiest way is to create the life we want to live in our mind's eye so clearly that our mind experiences it as reality. Did you know your mind can't determine if your daydream is reality or not? We have that much power. I began imagining myself running again. I could feel the wind on my face, the sweat on my hairline, and the feeling of my feet on the road. I envisioned this over and over. When I first started imagining this, I really wasn't sure if it was possible. The more times I ran through it in my mind's eye, the more I believed it would happen. I focused on what my five senses would be experiencing and made the experience come to life. I would fall asleep envisioning myself hiking, running, swimming, or playing sports with my kids. I would do exercises that I could do currently to strengthen my muscles and work toward these health goals. The first time I ran again after a four-and-a-half-year break it was like no time had passed. I had spent the better part of the last year envisioning it over and over. I actually felt like I could have run a lot more than I allowed myself to for the first two weeks! That's the power of the mind. When you can get your mind and your body on the same team, nothing can stop you from healing, from accomplishing every goal you have set for yourself.

It is your innate ability to heal, not only because of the wisdom of your body but because of your connection to God. You are more powerful than you even can imagine. I believe that healing is your birthright.

CHAPTER 25

I Am Worthy

I initially thought this chapter was about being worthy of healing, but that is not what I am being inspired to write. Now, God is saying it is about knowing your worth for the work you have been called to do. There may be some overlap among your feelings of being worthy to heal, worthy of your calling, worthy of your purpose. So let these words speak to you where you are right now in your life. **Let God mold these words to be spoken to you.**

For much of my life I have struggled with knowing my worth. I don't know if this came from abuse at a young age or fearing the power I felt inside of me that I was being called to own. Then it carried over to believing I was not worthy of complete healing, not worthy of this amazing man I married, not worthy of money or success.

All these are LIES.

This week, I have begun to understand and know my worth at a deeper level. Do not let this fool you. This does not mean I'll never struggle with my worth again. It just means I know my worth right now and when doubt comes knocking, I will not invite it in!

If feeling worthy seems foreign to you—whether it's due to your religious upbringing, your humanness, ego, or self-doubt—let's challenge that belief system a bit. What if instead of saying, "I am not worthy of all God has to offer me," we say, "What if I am worthy?"

This takes your mind from a place of keeping you safe from disappointment and danger and lets it start to tease out the idea of being worthy.

What law says you aren't worthy? I sure haven't found one.

I think we overcomplicate this concept. What is worth, anyway?

What if *worth* is really just understanding who God sees you as? What if *worth* is seeing yourself as God sees you?

Take a deep breath and try that one on.

If the idea of this kind, loving God does not fit into your worldview of Him yet, I ask that you just don't push this away. Just sit with it. Lean into why it makes you uncomfortable, and you may find it leads to an experience that actually started this belief of, "I'm not worthy."

Stop speaking this belief into existence. From now on, every time you hear the doubt, I want you to repeat this:

> *I am worthy.*

I AM WORTHY

I am worthy.

I am worthy.

Be okay to take up space. If you are reading this book, you most likely have felt oppressed in some way, or told you're too much, and it caused you to shrink down to make others feel comfortable. Do not live life under that type of oppression. You may not have seen it through that lens before now.

Be willing to get uncomfortable in the process of being comfortable taking up space again. Know you were meant to own that space. Be the person who changes the energy when you walk into a room. Know that it is a gift, and stop trying to dim that light to make others feel comfortable. Get used to getting uncomfortable, for it is in that discomfort that we begin to harness all we are worthy of.

When taking up space and being seen is new, make sure you only share on fertile ground until you have more confidence. Only share within safe friendships, or with life coaches or therapists who will speak life into your future self.

As you move forward, remember that recognizing your worth is a journey, not a destination. It's about embracing who you are with all your strengths and flaws and understanding that you are inherently valuable. You are not defined by your past, your doubts, or the voices that have told you otherwise.

Start to live in the truth that you are worthy—worthy of healing, love, success, and everything good that comes your way. You don't need to shrink yourself to fit into the world around you. Instead, allow yourself to expand, to fill the space you were always meant to inhabit.

This process might feel uncomfortable at times, but that's where growth happens. As you challenge old beliefs and step into your true worth, remember to protect your energy and share your journey with those who will uplift and support you. Surround yourself with people who see your worth and help you see it too.

Let this be your new mantra: **I am worthy.** Say it often, believe it deeply, and live it fully. The world needs you to be exactly who you are—nothing more, nothing less. So take up space, shine your light, and know that you are deserving of every good thing that comes your way.

CHAPTER 26

Growth

Growth sucks. It is uncomfortable. I think of the work a baby chick has to do to pip the eggshell and break out of it. If you help the chick, you are really not doing it any favors. By breaking out of its shell, the chick learns vital life skills to help it adapt to its surroundings. If you help the chick, you hinder its ability to survive and thrive.

Growth is much like a seed in the ground, buried in the dark, wet soil. The sun can't reach it yet, but it feels the warmth of her rays and uses the water to soften its outer shell. Peaking out of the seed, the stem begins to unfold toward the warmth of the sun, finally breaking through the surface of the soil to feel the enchanting rays of the sunshine. If this baby plant has too much direct sun in the early days it will fry, shrivel up, and die. Just as some people notice and dislike the crack in the soil when a plant pushes through to grow, there will be those around you who are uncomfortable with your growth. They might think you're disrupting the status quo and wonder, "What was wrong with the way things were before? Everything was smooth!" They may not recognize the beauty in your growth.

I encourage you to be mindful of who you share your growth with, where you plant your dreams, and who you allow to nurture them. The people you surround yourself with will either nourish your growth or hinder it. Choose wisely, as they can either help your potential flourish or stunt it before it has a chance to thrive.

We were not designed to stay stagnant. We were not made to make others comfortable. Beware of those who no longer should be in your circle. There are times we have outgrown people in our lives and we need to be smart enough to know when to walk away from them.

Growth does take work, but it does not need to be forced. It takes intention and feels icky most of the time. On the other side of growth is freedom. There is featherlike lightness to it. There is healing.

Like plants experience each season differently, so do we experience seasons in life, and what we need in each season changes. In winter, a bulb needs the insulation of the ground to protect it so that it can bloom again in the spring. In the winter, there is no evidence of those bulbs under the crest of the earth. If you didn't plant them there yourself, or see the flowers from them last year in spring, you would not know of their existence.

GROWTH

In the spring, a bulb needs the warmer days to wake it back up to life from its slumber, but it was its slumber that nourished the bulb to allow it to grow into such a vibrant part of life, full of color and joy. It provides beauty and peace to those who walk past it. It provides pollen for the bees and nectar for the hummingbirds. Without the season of rest it could be and do none of those things.

Know when it is your season of rest.

Growth is not a 24-7 process. Sometimes growth comes in the resting, in the being still, in allowing others to nourish our souls. Invest in things that nourish your soul: retreats, webinars, personal development programs, masterminds. Embrace each season with the knowledge that it has a purpose. Sometimes the purpose is to refill, and sometimes the purpose is sharing your beauty and growth.

I think it is important to know that throughout growth, we have to let go of parts of us or our lives that don't serve us anymore. That may come in the form of disconnecting from Facebook groups, friendships, business relationships. Like a snake shedding skin, these are necessary parts of growth. Without them, you will not grow; you will shrink back down to fit a skin that no longer serves you.

For me, this realization came through the people I followed on social media who identified as chronic illness warriors. If they weren't embracing hope for healing, encouraging it, or sharing uplifting messages, I realized they were no longer serving me. I needed to leave groups that felt there was no true healing possible for a genetic disorder because I had found hope in them at one point, but they were keeping me sick now.

To focus on healing, I had to shift what I listened to, from the conversations I had with friends I spoke with regularly to podcasts I was listening to. If the messages I was telling myself and my body did not line up with what messages, energy, and conversations I was holding, then all the work I had put into healing was being canceled out. I have come too far to be afraid of letting go of things that don't serve me anymore that make me stay sick. Nothing is worth me staying sick for. If you have experienced chronic illness in any depth, you understand this statement. It doesn't make letting go any less difficult, but it is part of the sacrifice of growth. Much like training for a marathon, you will, for a while, perhaps change your exercise routine, how you fuel your body, and what you do for your strength training. All for a season. After you run your race, you may choose to eat foods you excluded for a while, or you may not.

Don't look at any loss as absolute. Know you are in a season of growth, healing, and rest and what you consume is important right now. Protect those seeds. That is the hope of your future, of the life you were meant to live and are being called to live. Be courageous and show others that healing is possible.

GROWTH

There's an aspect of growth that I don't hear people talk about often. In fact, I was surprised when I experienced it myself. At first I thought I was depressed, but that didn't fit quite right. My nervous system was confused. I walked through the motions of my favorite day of the week, Thursday, with no spark. It's like I couldn't wake up my brain. I hadn't felt like this in a long time.

"What is wrong with me?"

I lay diagonally across my bed and opened up my journal. This page held a snapshot of my reality, where I am today—from my weight to the amount in my bank account. I flipped the page over and on this page I wrote my dreams:

This is what I want: the goal weight, the number of books I want to publish, the amount I want to make each month—down to how I want my relationships with those around me to be, how many intentional dinners I want, to the number of vacations a year with my boys and also just my spouse.

This page came all too easily to me. It was almost second nature to dream again. A year ago I could hardly dream. I was so stuck in my prison of chronic illness. I was merely hoping I could begin to hope again, and now I can dream and make this beautiful future in my mind as if it's my current reality.

Don't feel disheartened if you struggle to dream. Dreaming feels dangerous in the beginning. Your mind can't fathom how to think out of the daily life it knows. Your body warns you to keep safe. Don't push the status quo. What we know now is familiar. Comfortable. Dreaming of a better future is not.

This is my call today, to teach you to dream. I know dreaming may feel impossible in the beginning. You may not be in the prison of chronic illness, but you may be in another prison that has placed ceilings and walls around you, killing that part of you that dares not hope for it to change because getting your hopes up once again would be too painful. I understand that fear. I invite you to embrace that fear, not as a sign of danger but as old coding. Tell yourself its old coding. That's all. Thank it for showing up and allow it to pass. By honoring it with gratitude we can move through the emotions that paralyze us in the beginning. Then we begin to push the boundaries of dreaming.

It may be as simple as a walk in your yard, or as grand as meeting a friend for lunch, or even grander—a vacation with your family. Or it could be as simple as running errands again, such simple tasks others take for granted.

This weird depression-like feeling I have in my chest and head is grief. I'm mourning the old me as she dies. She has to. That Brooke can no longer serve me. She was the badass survivor; that was all she had to be to get me to this place—the place I write to you from—but she is not the one who can grow to be the person who walks onto stages, leads retreats, or hosts masterminds. I love the old Brooke fiercely. I'm so proud of her, and for once I don't need anyone else to be proud of me. My own pride is enough. I am enough.

Thank you. Thank you to me for bringing myself this far. Thank you to the one who was fearless, bold, and brave enough to challenge the system.

Thank you for making way for the new me to be birthed from the ashes and reborn like a phoenix.

CHAPTER 27

Authenticity = Safety and Healing

The humming of the bee was so distracting. I couldn't hear God over the noise! Then I heard God within the buzzing. I leaned into the music of the bees. The pink bush of flowers was tucked just behind the bench I was perched on. Then, in my mind's eye, I saw this bee return to the hive. The bee lives in the community. Each bee has a role in the function of the hive, but none does anything alone. The interesting thing about honey bees is together, as a community, they are healing. Together, their buzzing can heal PTSD. Together, the air from their hive can be healing for a human to breathe in, but alone, as a single bee, there is not enough quantity. It is the community of bees just doing bee things that is healing. The buzzing of their work, the air of the hive—the authenticity is the power in the community.

Authenticity is the highest frequency emotion. It is what draws in your people with a *Holy Hell Yes!* and propels others away. For so long I was lost, not understanding what authenticity really was. I did not realize that I had spent my whole life as a chameleon, always fitting into the boxes others created for me. As a chameleon I often became a mirror for the other person to make them comfortable. My authenticity was hidden. When you know you are a chameleon, that can be used as a gift to see others and hold space for them without mirroring their experience or expectations.

At my dad's house, I always did the grocery shopping with my stepmom, even when I really didn't want to because somewhere along the way I was pegged once as "the daughter who could outshop anyone." This didn't even make sense to me. I hate the store. I do not like shopping. I never have. There is no such thing as retail therapy for me, yet I was the girl who "loved" shopping.

At my mom's house I mostly just tried to do everything right. I thought if I did everything right, it would be easier for her as a single mom. I held my emotions in tight. I boxed them up real pretty so they wouldn't be noticed. I found refuge among horses. I found my love for horses at age six or seven. I understood them and they understood me. I could speak nothing and the horse knew how I was feeling. I found I could let go of any mask I had put on that day and just be me. That truly was my only experience with being authentic.

School was my safe place, but even there I wasn't authentic. I was exactly what I needed to be. I listened to the teacher to a T. I asked clarifying questions and not any stupid ones. At least, I didn't ask what I thought they would deem stupid. I loved math because math came more naturally to me and I could be smarter, but English was so hard. The English language is still a mystery to me, which is why it is so comical that God would have me write a book.

I have started this book so many times, never sure how it would end up. I look back now and think, *No wonder I couldn't write it. I was a chameleon, and there is no way on God's green earth I can be a chameleon and write a book on authenticity, healing, and overcoming.*

So, I began to break down the walls I had put up thinking they were keeping me safe from others. The most vital information I learned about myself was that others saw me as unapproachable. This is a problem for a psychology student. I was shocked to hear this. Offended even. After I learned this, over the course of the weeks that followed, I began to understand what people meant by that. Being a chameleon and fitting in everywhere was not doing me any favors. I thought people liked me but really, nobody knew me. *I didn't even know myself.*

And so I began to do the work. Sitting with this new realization, I took a deep breath in, starting in my womb and then expanding to my chest, filling my lungs completely. Although this breathwork session was slower than what I was used to, I noticed my body struggling—not in a nervous system way but in a way that felt safe this time. In the past, breathwork brought up fear: fear of passing out, triggering PTSD, or facing flashbacks. But this time was different; I felt safe in my body. Yet, despite this sense of safety, my spirit felt like it was fighting to take its first breaths again after my near-death experience. It felt contradictory—how could I feel like I was fighting for life, yet also feel so safe?

And I heard a message. The message is in the healing—not the actual physical healing I have done but the emotional healing I have done to be a safe vessel for my spirit. Over time, I have had to develop trust with MYSELF to find safety.

My body began to speak to me. The pain in my neck is from holding back. I have healed so much, but I have not spoken about it. Now I choose to speak with authenticity. No hiding, no holding back. Now I am ready to heal, physically and emotionally. I speak to heal.

This may seem like a new point of view . . . but LEAN into this. I find that it's so interesting that I have a physical ailment: a cervical fusion and neck injury. Yet, I still wonder if I would suffer from neck pain even without these issues. I'm beginning to realize that my suffering might be tied to keeping my voice silent, holding back what I need to express. I've had visions at times, and some of the earliest ones from when I was a teenager showed me as a speaker. Back then, I had no idea what I would even talk about. After having kids, I nearly forgot about this dream of public speaking as I became entirely focused on what I believed was my life's mission: raising tiny humans.

After my postpartum psychosis, I started seeing myself on stages again, this time much bigger than before. It scared me. I thought that I could never be that person who could be so bold as to speak in front of so many people and share such intimate details of my life. Now, after years of neck pain and wearing a brace, I can see myself becoming that person I once envisioned. But I still don't fully understand how it will happen. How can I, with my physical conditions, get on a stage and speak? How can I, someone who has just fought to survive, step into that role?

I never used to make plans. Not really. They were tentative plans. If the weather behaves and I don't have a migraine, if my pain level isn't overriding me that day, then we can meet up for dinner. Then we can go on a walk. If not, then I can't. How many times do we live stuck in the mud of this? I know I am not the only one. I couldn't see how I would do it because I am human.

Now, through more healing, I am understanding. I am seeing. What I didn't see then was the level of healing that was possible. I was putting a ceiling on myself. I was not yet surrounded by a high frequency community of authentic leaders to speak life into my soul in a way that helped me challenge my own beliefs on healing. I used to think healing meant reaching a daily pain level 3, not needing to rest in the afternoon, and being able to work as a therapist. But now I realize this definition was still playing small. When I was very chronically ill, even that level of healing seemed out of reach. However, as I got closer to that level of healing, I became more aware of my circle of friends and consciously started surrounding myself with bold, life-giving, high-frequency people. This shift in my environment changed my belief in what healing could be. I began to dream bigger, have more faith, and push my healing beyond what I once thought possible.

Now on an average day, my pain scale is less than 2. Even after I go for a run, my pain scale in my neck is low. Migraines rarely hit. I am beginning to rarely be affected by storms that used to for sure, 100% of the time, knock me out and keep me in bed.

I do think I could have eventually gotten to this point on my own, without the community, but it would have been slow progress. Authentic, life-giving community compressed time for me in healing.

Do not panic if you don't have these types of people in your life, yet. They will come if you shift your energy. When they do, they will help compress time in your healing. Until then, you can and will see miracles every day. You will, especially if you start acknowledging them. I just want you to see the power of being authentic and surrounding yourself with an authentic community. This is what God intended for our lives. This is the village you are meant to be in.

CHAPTER 28

Waiting to be Healed to Live

Stop waiting to be healed to live.

You can do both.

Nobody told you could do both.

Let the living heal you!

Stop saying *someday*. Do it now. Live now. *Living* will be the medicine that heals you.

The belief that you have to wait until you are healed to live is the toxicity that is keeping you stuck, keeping you sick, keeping you in the prison you've created, and living is the key that unlocks it!

I had forgotten how to dream. Isn't that interesting? Now, as I reflect on my journey, I realize I have gained agency over my migraines, and I know I have the power to use my voice.

Yet, when it comes to something as simple as planning a romantic getaway, I can't even imagine where to go because I've stopped living and dreaming for so long!

It's like constantly checking to make sure all your limbs are intact but never actually using them for what they were meant to do. What if we stopped looking down and started looking up?

Looking down, all you see is the ground. You don't see what's coming. You don't see the sky, the birds flying. It is like you had no idea creatures could fly so high because all you saw were the ants crawling on the dirt.

Look up! Begin to dream again, especially when it is hard and scary to do so. This will be the sweetest medicine to your soul. Picture yourself healthy, living out this trip, walking the beach hand-in-hand with someone you love, finding little secret hideaways to just be, watching the sunrise with a cup of coffee in your hand. Celebrate the life you've been given.

In waiting to live until you are healed you will wake up one day to realize you let your whole life pass you by. You are stuck in chronic illness because you are just trying to survive the day . . . to survive. Let go of this! It does not serve you.

Make the plans for lunch.

Make plans for the date.

Book the trip!

You will find that sometimes the radical act of trusting with faith results in divine healing to the body.

The act of living contradicts the frequency of being stuck, stagnant in chronic illness. The two cannot coexist together.

Where one flourishes the other dies. Which seed are you watering?

This chapter may not actually be about chronic illness for you. This may be about being stuck in the wrong relationship or the wrong job. Let these words carry meaning for you still.

To break free from your prison, to unlock the door, the key is to live. Begin to act on your dreams!

You can heal AND live. Doing so is the antidote to the poison you are drinking.

Let the words on this page be your lifeline. Don't dismiss the difficult messages because the lifeline was not what you expected.

Right now, you are drowning and my words may not be the lifeline you expected. You may be saying to God:

God, I'm drowning. Please help me!

But not by simply letting me climb into a stranger's boat; that's too easy. Life isn't supposed to be that easy.

And not by learning from someone else's lessons; that's not for me. I need to find my own path, to face my own challenges. So I stay in suffering.

It's interesting how we dismiss God's help when it doesn't show up the way we expect. We want a quick fix, but God often offers us a chance to grow instead.

I waited in faith, hoping God would just heal me, take away the pain and struggle. But instead, He wanted me to learn how to own my voice, to discover my strength through the journey.

I know that we want to be healed. And we want life to look a certain way. We expect God to answer our prayers in the exact way we ask for them to be answered. But sometimes God heals us in ways we could never imagine. All you need to do is ask and have faith. Have faith that God will guide you through your healing journey.

Some things I say might not sit right with you, and that's okay. Just be aware that if you're pushing it away, it might be because it feels uncomfortable or because you believe it doesn't apply to you.

Is it the discomfort of being called out that feels unsettling? I've noticed that when someone says something that resonates with me, but I'm not quite ready to embrace it, I sometimes feel a bit resistant, as if I want to dismiss the message. Often, that's just my ego trying to protect me and keep me in my comfort zone. By staying stuck my ego thinks it is safe, and it is not. Don't let your ego keep you stuck or sick. Take what I am writing to God, to your knowing, and see where you start, what you keep, what you put aside for later. There are many parts to digest in this book and I don't expect anyone can do it in one go. Just don't dismiss the lifeline because it's not the message you *wanted* from God.

CHAPTER 29

Phoenix Rising from the Ashes

I can't just survive this for me but for others. This theme has repeated itself in my life since I was a young girl. God has called me to this work of sharing a message of HOPE. He prepared me at a young age to want to use all my experiences for expansion, for compassion, for reaching others.

"All we need is hope, and for that we have each other."[3] Andra Day sang those words.

They give me chills. Because I know them to be true.

I've said it before and I will say it again: My healing in all areas of my life does not make me special. It does not make me magical. It does not make me unique. It literally means that it is a law that you, too, can rise up and find healing.

---

[3] "Rise Up," written by Andra Day and Jennifer Decilveo, performed and recorded by Andra Day, released by Warner Music Group, track 2 on *Cheers to the Fall*, August 28, 2015.

I know it is hard to believe that healing is possible for you. I know that it is easier to stay in the illness that feels safe to you. I know that there is fear in believing what I am telling you, but I believe it to be true because I lived it. I lived it and I *do* live it, and I believe it is possible for you to live it too.

Have you ever taken lyrics to an anthem song and just highlight what speaks to you and black out all the rest? It sounds weird, but it's like just highlighting the affirmations for your life.

Here are a few lines from a song that speak to me for you.

> *And you can't find the fighter*
> *But I see it in you so we gonna walk it out*
> **—Andra Day, "Rise Up"**

I know you don't see the fighter in you. Maybe you've never had someone to believe in you. I see it in you. I know you're thinking, *Brooke, you don't know me.* **Yes, I do.** I have seen you in my heart all week. You have lived this book with me. You have been in my energy field. You have been in my dreams and visions. I KNOW the fighter in you. Everyone who faces really hard things has survived 100% of the days they've lived, and that took a fighter.

Now it is time to lay down survival mode and rise up to living life!

> *I'll rise up*
> *In spite of the ache*

> *I'll rise up*
> *And I'll do it a thousand times again*
> *For you*
>
> **—Andra Day, "Rise Up"**

I have risen up from the ashes, over and over again—each time not the same person I was before. Each time I have risen up a new me. You may see these experiences as brokenness. I did too. Then I saw what it meant to be broken. In our brokenness, our weakness, we are whole. That is where expansion comes from. What if we were never meant to be fixed? What if the brokenness is the key to living life fully, *even with*?

Even with . . .

Live, even with . . . don't fight the pain, don't fight the darkness. Let the brokenness of these experiences lead you to the expansion of your soul. What if you let your brokenness liberate you to the expansion of fully living?

> *All we need, all we need is hope*
> *And for that we have each other*
> *And for that we have each other*
> *And we will rise*
>
> *. . .*
>
> *And we'll rise up*
> *High like the waves*

We'll rise up
In spite of the ache
We'll rise up
And we'll do it a thousand times again
—**Andra Day, "Rise Up"**

Remember how important community is. Remember the hope found in each other. Let this book not cause comparison between our lives. Let this book fill you with the overwhelming feeling of hope for your future.

I know that you have lived so long without hope. I know you have felt like *what is the point of even trying again; I'll just get knocked back down. Why do I hope, just to have it ripped out from under me?*

I know the pain of this feeling all too well. I have spent days in bed crying out to God, when His silence is deafening. Sometimes the silence distracts us from His presence. Sometimes He shows up in our lives as angels in human form saying, "**I have enough belief for the both of us.** Until you can believe in yourself enough, borrow some of my belief. Lean on mine. I have you." Let the community hold you much as my community has held me here this week.

You have a choice. You always have a choice. Using your voice to ask for what you want is like harnessing the full power of agency. My chronic illness took me out to teach me that. Don't be discouraged when the chronic illness comes talking. You hit "block" on that imaginary cell phone and let it know with your vibrations you have a new community holding you up, one of hope, frequency of miracles, and love. Love, the purest form of love for yourself, will be the most amazing healing medicine you could ever drink. It is like nectar for your soul.

Have you ever heard of kintsugi? It is the Japanese art form of repairing broken pottery. The broken pieces have gold glue applied to them. Then the pottery becomes stronger than before it was broken. The glue allows the pottery to become more durable, and that could only happen because it was broken first.

Think of that gold glue that holds the pieces back together as the love and expansion of self. The more gold glue there is, the more beautiful it is deemed. You, my friend, are rising up each time as a phoenix with more gold in your veins, more expansion, more love, more you.

You can *use* everything for your good. Do not confuse this with *it being* for your good: *it* being depression, mental illness, chronic illness, grief, loss, sickness, abuse. They are not *for your good*, but *you can use them* to fuel your fire for life, to add more gold to your veins, to be the fire that births the new phoenix within.

Let this book stretch you out of your comfort zones. Let it be a wake-up call to your soul to find your purpose. I know a life full of possibilities awaits you! A life that is fearless, a life full of living every dream you could have ever imagined. A life of you stepping into your divine power. A life of you using your voice to harness the power of agency and choosing to claim your purpose and power in this world.

Don't waste another day in unbelief! Don't wait. Work awaits you. You are a creator, and you can create any life you want. Remember, our bodies were designed to fully heal and it is our ego that must die to get out of the way. Let that ego burn in the ashes, and leave it behind, and you will be reborn as a new phoenix. With each fire let more of the ego be left behind until you are your highest frequency self—authentic, full of love, hope, and freedom. Chronic illness has no power over you anymore. Abuse holds no place in your life anymore. Your frequency has outgrown all of it. So let it be so.

This book may feel like tough love, but don't mistake it for a lack of compassion. I have deep compassion for you, and that's exactly why I need to speak and write these words. God has called me to speak and write these words, so that those who are ready to hear them, those who have heard the call, those who just need the path to be blazed before them *can enter into it.*

The road to healing can be lonely. It will make others uncomfortable. You are disrupting the patterns. You are disturbing people's roles in your life. They may try to keep you stuck, play the victim, or be mad about your healing. Know that this is part of the journey. Find yourself new people with higher frequency to match your new vibrations of life. It may take time, but you will be surprised that eventually your group of people will change. This is the coolest experiment I have ever done on purpose: inviting only people into my life who encourage growth, who hold space for healing, who speak the hard truths to me as I am to you. These are the people your future self needs. Welcome them in with open arms and know when you have outgrown someone.

I want you to know I am proud of you. And I invite you to be proud of yourself as well. You have walked through many fires in your life, and you are still here. You have faced pain many could never imagine. And you are still here. You sat with me and my words and now you have a choice. As you close this book, you get to choose: what life do you want to live? Choose it and then live it.

As we come to the end of this journey together, I want to leave you with a blessing, a blessing that will leave you with peace, love, and assurance that everything is going to work out exactly as it needs to.

Close your eyes and take a few deep cleansing breaths, and let these words find their way into your heart.

> *God wants you to know He sees you.*
> *He is not silent.*
> *He lives within you.*
> *Your experiences can be used for a purpose.*
> *He pours healing over you.*
> *Like a light from heaven coming over your head and down your entire body until not a section isn't touched by this*

Divine light.
Breathe it in.
Let it fill the cracks still aching for the purest love.
God has you in the palms of His hands.
He is so involved in your life that His fingerprints have been left all over it. Don't doubt that.
May you find the loving God I have come to know.
May you begin anew with Him.
Go in His peace and love.

And all God's people said,
Amen.

As you close this book, remember that your journey doesn't have to end here. I invite you to join me in a supportive community where you can continue to grow, heal, and discover your true potential. Together, we can walk this path, and you don't have to do it alone.

Within this community, you'll find the tools, resources, and programs designed to guide you through every step of your healing journey. Whether you need extra support, encouragement, or a space to connect with others who understand what you're going through, this is a place where you can thrive.

Take the next step with me and allow yourself to be supported as you continue to unfold the beautiful story of your life. You are worthy of all the healing and growth that lies ahead, and I'm here to help you every step of the way.

Join me today and let's continue this journey together.

Made in the USA
Las Vegas, NV
04 December 2024